THE
CONSERVATIVE
ECONOMIC
WORLD VIEW

The Ideal Worlds of Economics

THE CONSERVATIVE ECONOMIC WORLD VIEW

BENJAMIN WARD

Basic Books, Inc., Publishers   *New York*

Library of Congress Cataloging in Publication Data

Ward, Benjamin N
  The ideal worlds of economics.

  Includes bibliographies and index.
  CONTENTS: book 1.   The liberal economic world view.
—book 2.   The radical economic world view.—book 3.
The conservative economic world view.
    1.   Comparative economics.   2.   Liberalism.
3.   Marxian economics.   4.   Conservatism.   I.   Title.
HB90.W37   330   78–54497
ISBN: 0–465–03199–4
ISBN: 0–465–03926–X (v. 1) pbk.
ISBN: 0–465–06818–9 (v. 2) pbk.
ISBN: 0–465–01396–1 (v. 3) pbk.

Contents

PART I
The Optimal Conservative Economic World View

PART II
Commentary

ACKNOWLEDGMENTS

It is not so easy for a Berkeley economics professor to find a conservative with whom to talk over the issues. However, a certain number of conservative students have drifted into my classes, and some have gone out of their way to continue my education. I am particularly grateful to Paul Craig Roberts for a variety of such efforts over the years. An early interest in public choice theory has provided a number of opportunities for discussions with conservative economists. A semester of teaching at the University of Washington was both delightful and very useful. I am indebted to a helpful critic and friend, R. Joseph Monsen, for this opportunity, and also to Dwight Robinson and Trudy Murray, from whom I have learned much. Finally, I would like to thank Andrjej Brzeski of the Davis campus of my home university, a fine friend who offered a large number of penetrating criticisms of an earlier draft of the present work. Remaining failures to grasp conservative principles are, of course, my own.

PART I

The Optimal Conservative Economic World View

CHAPTER 1

Introduction

ONE OF the ironic events of recent years has been the furor over the hiring of radical economists in some of the leading economics departments in the United States. The irony stems from the fact that many of the best-known departments already had radicals among their faculty members. Far scarcer in most departments were conservatives; indeed, a number of the highest status departments had no conservatives at all on their faculties.

Radical rhetoric and threat did in fact produce results; well-meaning liberals found ways to make appointments based de facto on a political test despite the violation of rules, perhaps even of the Constitution, that was involved. But probably this success will be short-lived, not because the radicals can also be thrown out for political reasons, though that could happen, but because they really have very little to offer economics beyond rhetoric and threats. Propinquity in this case can only breed contempt.

But what then of those absent conservatives? The truth is that conservatism is having a rather profound effect on economics, even though it has been poorly represented in many research-oriented institutions. This effect is being exercised through the competition of ideas rather than by physical confrontation. Conservatives have been in the forefront of the reappraisal of Keynesian economics, and the reappraisal has already led to substantial modifications of the doctrine as it was being so confidently asserted only a dozen years ago. Some of the most interesting developments in the new field of public choice theory are the product of conservative thinkers; indeed, it would not be far off the mark to say that the field of public choice was created by conservatives. And perhaps the most interesting new slant on economics in recent years, the burgeoning property-rights literature, is unquestionably a conservative product. These conservative ideas, since they are clearly meeting the competitive tests of an ideologically unfriendly but still open environment, will be around long after the radical confrontationists have been returned to the street-corner intellectualism that seems to be their natural habitat.

Though the above-mentioned developments have their dimensions of originality, the basic principles of conservatism are by no means new. They have grown by evolution and have been tested in generations of experience. They differ from liberal and radical views in four fundamental ways. In the first place, the conservative rejects utopian and mechanistic "solutions" to human problems. Second, conservatism is based on recognition of the individual human being as the primary element in society. Third, the conservative identifies the family as the most important social unit in human society. And finally, conservatives believe that the provision of order is an essential task of government, without which the economy cannot provide opportunities for families and individuals. A conservative interpretation of the operation of the contemporary economy will, of course, make frequent use of these primary distinguishing features of conservatism. In the remainder of this chapter the aim will be simply to explain why these principles do in fact serve to distinguish conservative from liberal and radical thoughts.

The libertarian bias of the conservative is by now generally recognized in the United States. However, the basis of the emphasis on freedom as a fundamental value is often misunderstood. For as John Stuart Mill pointed out, the most effective arguments are negative ones. Mill argued that the individual is generally the best judge of what is best for himself, partly because he knows more about his own wants than others and partly because he cares more about them than do others. The implication of the argument is that individuals are possessed of a considerable amount of self-concern, and that this self-concern is combined with a considerable degree of material self-interest. These are hardly revolutionary notions, given that they are being asserted of an organism that can neither thrive nor even survive without regular and *individual* access to a variety of material objects, including most notably food. Add one more ingredient, namely, that there are not enough of those material objects to go around, that they are scarce, and the stage is set for a good conservative analysis of the functioning of human society.

Radicals, of course, deny the relevance of these points. That an individual should exhibit a high degree of self-concern is, for a radical, a sign not of normal functioning of an animal organism but of sickness. Radical intellectual leaders before the revolution, and political leaders after, continually assert their right to speak for others, to decide what is good for whom, and to suppress dissent on the subject whenever possible. And much of their argumentation even denied the existence of scarcity. For a century now Marxists have been denouncing scarcity economics without having anything to put in its place. They used to argue that socialist societies, by abolishing the wastes of capitalism, would almost automatically be societies of abundance. When that thesis was tested and the truth was found to be closer to the exact opposite, there was put in its place a good deal of talk about creating abundance by abolishing the desire for goods!

Radicals differ fundamentally and at every turn from conserva-

tives. But liberals, in their wishy-washy attempts to find a happy medium, are not actually so far behind the radicals. Big government in
Western Europe and the United States is the creature of liberal thought
and action. It is based on utopian and paternalistic notions of man. The
often incredible and genuinely uncountable direct interventions in human affairs that these monstrous concoctions carry out are justified by
liberals essentially on the grounds that the bureaucrat knows best what
is good for his client. But, in fact, the bureaucracy is not viewed as
confronting individuals directly. Everything is done on the basis of
averages and on the assumption of one group facing another, as in the
attempt to force poor neighborhoods to form groups, which would then
be given money to spend, assuming, of course, that the money will be
spent in ways that served to promote the best interests of the group
rather than the interests of its leaders. And as for scarcity, one need
only remember Galbraith's argument that Americans have far more
goods provided them by the market system than they ought to have,
and that they would be much better off if bureaucrats and politicans,
advised by the sage, made most of society's consumption decisions. At
times it seems as if the liberal were simply a more efficient kind of
radical, one who recognized that the goal of total state control was
more likely to be achieved if evolutionary rather than revolutionary
means were used.

Utopianism and a mechanistic approach to social policy tend to
go hand in hand. Much of the trouble that the American economy has
been in for almost a decade now has been a consequence of excessive
confidence in the products of the economist's art. Essential to the conservative's general position is the recognition of the complexity of the
human being and of his social relations. The consequences of any given
social policy cannot be predicted with much confidence, no matter how
sophisticated the mathematical model or the statistical manipulations
of the data. One of the basic ingredients of a conservative policy
toward economic stabilization is the recognition of this fact and a consequent attempt to limit the power of the government to foul things up
by limiting the power of government.

A radical cannot talk for more than five minutes about social reform without using words such as "solidarity" and "collective." Clearly,
the sooner individualism is eliminated, the happier the radical will be.
Liberals are a bit more subtle in their approach, but the result really is
not much different. Liberal social theory has virtually eliminated the
individual from consideration these days. Everything has to do with
the group. There is the interest group, the workplace group, the large
organization, small-group theory, and so on; the individual just doesn't
seem to be of much use these liberal days. Such general trends in social
theory find their reflection in economic model building, where the typical unit is the actor or agent, who can be an individual, a group, or
even a hierarchic organization. Furthermore, the models tend to assign
essentially the same traits to each "class" of actors, possibly with some
random variation thrown in. If you can find a few individuals in this
putative analogue of the real world, they will differ from one another

on, at best, a few well-specified and probably randomly distributed properties. And the outcomes, "efficient" or "optimal" though they may be, do not distinguish among this mish-mash of entities.

If liberal model building has strained out the individual, leaving either a collective or a very simple robot in his place, liberal social policy has substituted, at every turn, government-vs.-group interaction for the private bargains of the marketplace.

The twentieth century has seen perhaps the greatest assault on the family in recorded history. Socialists make no bones of their desire to destroy it; clearly, the family's cohesion gets seriously in the way of their designs for a more pliant individual. But liberals seem to have a similar notion. They often lead the discussion of the death of the family, treating its problems without reference to the fact that many of these same problems stem precisely from liberal social policy. One of the central functions of the family in history has been to serve as an institution of security. When the state becomes a substitute for the family as far as the material security of its members is concerned, this is bound to have a weakening effect. Compulsory features of the substitution leave the family bereft of one of its primary functions, whether its members like the idea or not. A second central function of the family has been the education of the child to fit him for the world. This function too is largely removed from family control through a massive public education system, supported by compulsory levies, in which the parents' ideas of education are given virtually no weight. And in the welfare system, as well as at a number of other turns in a family's history, the state bureaucrat is authorized to make deep interventions in family life, of which the systematic driving away of the male head of poor families is but one notorious instance. Other aspects of liberal society often force dependence onto the children until a late age, while depriving the parents of influence over their children. There is little wonder that after all this many liberal sociologists can make a comfortable living holding seminars on the decline of the American family.

Order is a concept that has very ambivalent meaning for a radical and, in practice at least, for the liberal as well. The atmosphere in which a revolutionary can flourish is one of disorder, and this, of course, serves to set his priorities. The disturbance of others in the exercise of their rights is the principal weapon of revolutionary change; the revolutionist has decided that he knows what's best for society and sets about to sow disorder through demonstrations, strikes, riots, agitation against the government, and so forth. We have described no ambivalence as yet—that emerges only after the revolutionary comes to power, when he suddenly feels the need for perfect "order" and sets about eliminating his enemies until he gets it. There will then be no more disorder in utopia until some comrades decide they want a different policy, and have the power to confront the new boss.

The liberal, on the other hand, carries his ambivalence with him at all times. Believing as he does that behavior that isn't nice only occurs because of the environment—in other words, that criminals and rioters are victims at least as much as those they are attacking—the liberal finds it very hard to call a halt by the use of force. The result is usually application of too little force and consequently a great deal more disorder.

The conservative position on these issues is very different. For a conservative, it is possible to draw a sharp line between orderly and disorderly behavior. The line drawing must be done carefully, but once it is drawn behavior toward those on the other side of the line should be quite unequivocal. The effort should involve effective deterrence through the use of overwhelming force and punishment as an indication that the individual *will* be held responsible for his acts in a free society.

As for the family, the conservative recognizes it as containing the deepest and most central relationships in an individual's life. The capacity to love is generated and expressed most profoundly in family relationships. But the family is also a very private institution, diverse and complex and still well beyond the grasp of social theory to comprehend. This fact plus its central place in society require support from society, not harassment. But given the historical inefficiency of the state in implementing policies of support, the strongest argument exists simply for saying, Hands off! to the state where family affairs are concerned. There is a very limited place for the state in regulating affairs among family members—essentially this role only occurs where family conflicts have spilled over into the outside world.

Individuals are no less complex than families. Their behavior too is not to be understood by simple models; nor is man well enough understood to be successfully manipulated into another kind of being by "instruments of social policy." Once again, what is needed is that he be left alone to seek his own way in the world, helped by his family and by his own efforts. And, once again, the essential role of government is to intervene only when these efforts have begun clearly to cause substantial harm to others. Family, freedom, and order are the unique basis of the conservative position.

CHAPTER 2

What Made the Modern World?

AN insufficiently noticed historical fact is that we tend to know more about those societies in which trading was a major activity than about others. We know a great deal about Athens, very little really about Sparta. Rome's history is shrouded in darkness in its earliest, traditional era of kingship and in the later period of attempted direct imperial control of the economy. The great trading period of the later republic and early empire provides us with substantial documentation. In the Middle Ages we have plenty of information about the great Italian trading cities, increasing information about Britain as she emerges as a trading nation, while much of the history of centralist Byzantium is blank. And in our own era what we know about Western market societies stands in sharp contrast to the few bits of information that filter out of closed socialist societies.

Of course, this is no accident. Merchants need information as a central part of their business. Furthermore, they need to supply information to prospective customers as a necessary part of making a sale. Much of what we think of as the organization of a market consists in ways of getting information to those who may want to deal on that market. But the need for information in order to do business goes deeper than this. Successful deal making requires that the trader acquire some understanding of the wishes and motives and resources of his prospective customer, if only so that he can use the information to get the best possible deal for himself. The market tends to develop in the successful trader a sensitivity to the wishes of others, and for the most durable of motives, namely, his own benefit. The old Fuller Brush man certainly was no philanthropist, and may at times have been something of a nuisance, but he did epitomize the market in this respect. Once he got your attention by coming around to you, he then made a genuine effort to find a match between your tastes and his wares. And the customer has, to some extent, an incentive to reveal his wishes; he too may want to bargain and to simulate those wishes, but if his wants are not known they are hardly likely to be satisfied on the market.

The contrast with bureaucratic societies is striking. There the leadership has a strong desire to know a number of things about its citizenry. But the great inequality between leader and led makes the citizen much more wary of revealing his wishes, especially any that may run counter to the leader's own ideas as to what is appropriate for the citizenry. The tax collector is not a person there is much incentive to expose one's wishes and resources to, and in a bureaucracy every bureaucrat is a tax collector, in the sense that he has the power to restrict the freedom of action of his clients, which is precisely what taking money from them does. In addition, the bureaucracy has very little incentive to provide information to outsiders, since it is too likely to reveal mistakes and can serve little positive purpose, at least from the bureaucrat's point of view. The Watergate events, clearly a product of big government, are the latest illustration of this aspect of bureaucracy.

Thus the greater informational openness of the trading society tends to be accompanied by a greater freedom of action for participants. Primarily, this is a consequence of the voluntary nature of deal making, the ability of each party to say, No deal! which is present so long as bargaining power is not too unequal. This openness tends in turn to promote mobility for the citizenry. Knowledge of opportunities elsewhere is one of the trader's main stocks-in-trade, and the information gets around. It is no accident that serfdom tended to be abandoned first in those parts of Europe in which trade was beginning to flourish, and that it persisted or was even recreated in those parts of Europe in which a strong centralized regime was able to prevent by force the rise of petty trade. Another reflection of this greater freedom of action and the trader's relation to information is manifested in the relation between trade and education. Many of our earliest written documents relate to trade, alphabets may have been initially designed for traders' use, and merchants have always been among the most important groups to acquire some measure of literacy. The need to keep records of business activity and to send letters in search of information about trading opportunities have thus been among the prime stimuli to the development of literacy.

The relation between trade and the development of industry has also been very close. Actually, the artisan is best viewed as a kind of trader. His shop is likely to lie alongside that of the trader, and he too has some portion of his clientele as regular customers to whose special wishes he caters and some portion of nonrepeat business. The artisan uses his knowledge and skill to process goods so as to enhance their value; so does the trader, but by selecting and moving them to the place where they are likely to be demanded. The processes of development of industry involved the trader at every turn. In this connection one need only mention that intermediate stage in development, the putting-out system, in which the merchant controlled a series of production processes, or the early factories, which were very often financed by merchant capital.

Trade opened up the world, introduced a strong element of voluntarism into economic life, and became a prime mover in the process of creating the modern world of industry and affluent, educated citizenries. It is probably the single most dynamic social process known to history. But that, of course, is not to say that it is perfect, only that it has established itself as a far better basis for much human interaction than any other known social process.

There are very strong biases against trade in both the liberal and radical literatures. The model of trading activity that is suggested is something like Cortez conquering and slaughtering the Aztecs. "Imperialism," "merchants of death," and a variety of other slogans are used to associate trade and wars in the reader's mind. In a way this is understandable, for the study of economic history was strongly under the influence of Marxism during most of the twentieth century. Only recently has a new economic history been developing that shows just how wrong these interpretations have been.[1]

The facts are almost the opposite of those depicted by liberal and radical historians. The merchant has a strong interest in an orderly environment, for only then can he bring his skills to bear in anticipating changes in demand and in economic values, which are the basis of his operation. A few examples will serve to illustrate the general point. Consider first the merchant corporations of early modern times, such as the East India Company, which represent the liberal archetype of the predatory merchant warmonger. The truth is that these merchants went into lands where there was already great disorder. They attempted at first to trade from the margins of those societies but found that the societies were too subject to random disorders for any durable trade relations to develop. At that point some of the merchant houses embarked on conquest of the land, assisted, of course, by their home government. But the aim was to bring order, and that in fact was what happened. Liberal and radical historians tell the exciting story of the war, but lose interest when the unexciting aftermath unfolds. For example, in the Indian case, it was merely assumed that as a result of conquest the Indian economy was gutted and starved for generations. We now know that to be false, and it seems that the higher level of public order brought by the colonists permitted substantial economic development in parts of colonial Africa and Asia, development that compares very favorably with the situation in those areas that remained "free" of colonial rule.[2]

The association between trade and freedom has historically been very close. We have already mentioned Athens and Britain. The United States is, of course, another example, where the impetus for the elimination of slavery came from merchant-dominated New England. And at the opposite end of the spectrum we see the very different nature of order under a despotic rule where trade is typically despised. In such places, from ancient Egypt to Ottoman Turkey, from Byzantium to the

Incas, the soldier, the priest, the bureaucrat is continually intervening in the affairs of the citizenry in arbitrary ways. The effects are clear enough: When the citizenry comes to understand that economic success will in all likelihood be siphoned off by some governmental hanger-on, the incentive to create economic successes wanes, and the regime slips into stagnation and decay. It is generally true in history that periods of flourishing economic activity and freedom tend to coincide with periods in which trade and the merchant are near the center of things and wars and bureaucrats in the background. This story is beginning once again to be told accurately in the literature of economic history.

In the nineteenth century a new kind of society emerged and began a process of relatively peaceful conquest of the world. This was the thoroughgoing trading society, and England and the United States were its proving grounds. The particularly novel feature of this form of society lay in the marketization of land, labor, and capital. In earlier times each of these factors of production had been subject to occasional sale from time to time, but never before had an integrated market system involving all three of the basic factors developed.

The process of development of trading societies was relatively peaceful, that is to say, very peaceful when compared with the histories of bureaucratic societies, but not without some measure of exciting times. Old values change slowly, and markets themselves are complex phenomena. Markets develop with experience in trading, with the emergence of a body of traders who understand how the market works, who know its facts, and who can pass on the hard-earned wisdom to succeeding generations. For each market has its pitfalls and risks, and the conservative trader, the one who wants to be able to continue trading year after year, must acquire the prudent insight that only this accumulated knowledge can provide.

An example from labor market history will illustrate this point. Radicals claim that the marketization of labor wreaked havoc on the economic condition of the workers, removing them from the protections of feudal or semifeudal agriculture and turning them into commodities, to be bought and sold like dead fish. However, the available facts suggest that the economic condition of workers generally was improved by the shift, there being strong evidence that movement into the marketized labor force was largely voluntary and involved short-distance migration. Consequently the worker probably did know something of the terms that were being offered him in both town and country, and so could make an informed choice. Nevertheless, some problems emerged, one of these obviously being the insecurity of life in the market, where in hard times the worker was likely to be laid off. Actually, even here the move to the labor market probably did more good than harm. The worker's level of insecurity may not have been greater than it had been on the farm; in many areas the incidence of bad crop years was even more frequent than the incidence of the business cycle in town, and often led to starvation for the peasant. But, more important, as the labor market developed and became organized, workers in similar situations found it feasible to develop their own job and sickness insurance. These so-called friendly societies took voluntary contributions from the workers and offered premiums when the worker fell on certain kinds of hard times. Thus the development of markets generated the opportunity for the development of voluntary insurance schemes by which workers could *protect themselves* against insecurity. In fact, as marketization spread to the countryside a similar phenomenon developed there too in the form of voluntary farm credit unions.[3]

The story of the rise of real wages in England and the United States is too well known to need repeating. The horror stories that have been told of the industrial revolution deal mainly with transient phenomena associated with the transition to marketization and with problems in declining industries. These problems have always been with us; *what the market system did was make the facts widely known.* In some few cases there was a good argument for limited government intervention. But there was never a case that on balance the condition of labor was worsened by the market system. Not only did the workers' real economic situation improve, but the market created opportunities for upward mobility for the more energetic that were far greater than history had known before. The openness of the society, its dynamic quality, and the structuring of energies in the direction of helping oneself by providing goods and services others were willing to make material sacrifices to obtain: These were the central ingredients of this new social form.

Clearly, the family is the most ubiquitous of history's social institutions. It comes in various forms, but at the heart of every form are parenthood and durable sexual relations. In the West in particular, and in trading societies in general, the conventional husband-wife, natural parent-child form of the family has been dominant. Less close ties of kinship often are reflected in cooperative relations for economic purposes, as in the extended family of agricultural and merchant fame.

Obviously, these relationships are the closest ones humans can have. That the conventional family has proved historically to be the dominant form for supporting central emotional needs speaks well of it as a basic social institution. But the family has also served other functions as well. Already mentioned has been its great significance as a private social-security institution. It has also often served as a support for more mobile members of the family. A common pattern of migration has the first established family member in the city create a sort of base to which later other family members can come in order to ease the burden of transition from country to city. Also familiar is the custom in poorer families of concentrating the family savings on giving a special advantage, such as professional education, to one member. In these and a number of other ways family relations have provided a secure base for further advance by members of the family, and not infrequently for the family as a whole.

Down to the nineteenth-century political history could be told essentially in terms of family relations, except perhaps in one or two of the largest of bureaucratic states. Political factions tended to be united around a central family and its clients or prospective beneficiaries. Once again the warmth of family relations served as a basis for alliance on the wider scene of political competition. Of course, that does not mean that there were never rifts within families, only that on the whole it proved to be the most secure amalgam for political alliance.

Throughout much of history larger economic units were essentially households, operating either as family farms or merchant businesses. In both cases a large number of hired or servile hands might be employed, but the central positions of influence within the unit would be family members, and the operation would tend to be headed by the family head. Some of the larger and more successful economic units have played a vital role in the development and testing of political institutions compatible with the thoroughgoing trading economy. Everyone knows the story of Magna Carta, the first great bill of rights growing out of resistance by aristocratic families to attempted usurpations of power by the king. Less well known these days, but of central historical significance, is the story of the organization of the Venetian state. An elaborate system of checks and balances was developed to prevent the ruler from acquiring the ability to dominate the other families in the ruling oligarchy, and this system may have been the model from which the American system of checks and balances ultimately was developed.

The great feudal landlords of England and the great merchant oligarchs of Venice headed powerful, autonomous, and self-concerned family businesses. Because of their autonomy and power, they played a central role in the historical development of the idea of a free society, though they represented transitional stages in that development. Their autonomy was based in part on the security of family relations, which gave the basic unit a cohesion and durability it could not otherwise have possessed.

Yet another influence of the family relates to its role in that most creative aspect of the thoroughgoing trading economy, namely, entrepreneurship. It appears that one of the central motivations energetic and creative people bring to the marketplace is the modern version of founding a dynasty. That is, they are motivated to found a fortune by the desire to have a durable and substantial legacy to pass on to their children. This is the one central respect in which the existence of families modifies the principles of individualism. At more modest levels of economic activity it is reflected in the sacrifices parents make for the education of their children, typically motivated by the desire to improve their economic chances in life. As one of the most important of motivations, inspiring, it should be emphasized, the expenditure of much energy in economic activity as well as "sacrifice," it is one of the most important sources of dynamism in society, a resource, if you like, that one would expect a free society to treasure and support.[4]

In summary, we see that the answer to the chapter's title question is the trinity noted at the end of chapter 1, namely, freedom, family, and order. But associated closely with each of these factors is the institution of the market and trade. The profit-seeking merchant needs freedom because his profits are often to be found in doing something different, in finding some opportunity neglected by others. The family has served as both means and end; on the one hand, it serves as a source of reliable colleagues in the economic venture, while at the same time the improvement of the material condition, status, and prospects of the family provides one of the most fundamental drives of the trader. And order is the environment within which markets serve their enabling functions most effectively, providing information and opportunity to the energetic seeker after profits, and satisfying the desires of those with both wants and means. In the next two chapters we look briefly at several societies where this trinity has served as a central basis for extraordinary achievement.

CHAPTER 3

Prosperity and Order in Ancient China and Republican Venice

THE libertarian conservative position is closely associated in the historical literature with a number of root facts and ideas. It is, of course, centrally related to the ideas of the British empiricist philosophers of the seventeenth and eighteenth centuries. It is associated with the rise of the laissez-faire economy in Britain and elsewhere in the nineteenth century. Both the notion of freedom and the association of freedom with trade go back to ancient Greece. And the association of trade and the rule of law suggests the Rome of the republic. These are familiar stories. However, they are often dismissed as being but a single, now irrelevant, story of the brief expansion of markets and development of ideas in small trading societies, whose occupation of history's center stage was always of short duration. The sense often conveyed is that the fragility of the societies is a disproof of the validity of the ideas.

In this chapter we try to combat this line of anticonservative thought by discussing the features of two societies whose history confounds the liberal or radical critic. Both were among history's most durable societies, preserving essentially similar regimes over a period of many centuries. Both provided a successful amalgam of economic and political order as the basis of their durability, and in both societies the family was fostered as a central social institution. As we will see, even in their demise are found lessons of importance for conservatism. And they show clearly the lack of time- and culture-dependence of major conservative principles.

The basic social structure of China was probably established about the time of Rome's great wars with Carthage, that is, a century or two before Christ.[1] This structure persisted through two thousand years of challenging and often violent history, and even today, under communism, it exerts a strong force. Conquest and invasion at several points broke up the existing society, but when some kind of order returned to the land the Chinese went right back each time to this traditional social structure. During much of its history Chinese society was very dynamic; when Marco Polo visited China in the thirteenth century, he observed a culture that clearly was more advanced than his own. Thus the basic Chinese social structure had survived dramatic technological transformations as well.

The secret of the Chinese success did not lie in Peking. Rather it lay in a peculiar arrangement that permitted a great deal of local autonomy. Recruitment to the Chinese national bureaucracy was by means of competitive examinations, given periodically and dealing with the classics of Chinese culture. Scions of the highest status families often were able to bypass the examinations, or at least most of them, but still the element of competition in the selection procedure was very strong. It also generated, uniquely in the world for much of its history, a literate bureaucracy, which of course greatly facilitated information flow to and from the center. The basic recruiting ground for this bureaucracy, however, was the local elite, often called the gentry. These were the richer—and as a rule the more powerful—families in a given district. Their sons would typically be given some education and might pass the earlier stage examinations even though they never entered the bureaucracy. This gave them some ties of sympathy and common experience with the bureaucrats, and was the source from which renewal of the system occurred after a time of troubles.

But contrary to widespread impression, the bureaucracy did *not* run the Chinese economy. The lowest level member of the national bureaucracy might typically be the sole representative of that bureaucracy in a district roughly comparable to an American county. Basic economic activity was carried on mostly in a highly decentralized way, agriculture, of course, being its base, but with trade present and in good times even flourishing. And even in its irrigation works China did not operate as a vast beehivelike "hydraulic society." Most irrigation works were small-scale projects, organized and carried out under local aegis. That vast bureaucratic superstructure was not essential to the survival of Chinese agriculture. Local society was largely controlled by the gentry, whose power stemmed both from their wealth and from their close contacts with the bureaucracy. In time of revolt they could, of course, call on the state for assistance, but in normal times this was not necessary to the economy's successful functioning. They raised crops on their own land, no doubt were often involved in moneylending, and provided the demand side of the market for many types of luxury goods.

The competitive and intellectually stimulating life of a bureaucrat kept his central interests focused internally on the bureaucracy and his and his friends' paths through it. One of the great virtues of the system was that in normal times the bureaucrats were too busy with their own concerns to pay too much attention to what was going on in the economy. Of course, they did provide a steady flow of tax revenue to the center to support themselves, their rulers' whims, and at times to provide for the national defense. But even this operation was often tempered by the typical bureaucrat's close ties of family with some locality, a past that gave him some feel for what the traffic would bear. And this feel was kept alive by the constant risks in his career, risks that meant he might at any time be sent back home, his bureaucratic career at an end.

The secret of Chinese society thus lay in the system of elite circulation, which provided for both stability and decentralization in a combination that has rarely been achieved in world history. The gentry appear as the primary element of stability, families whose claim to influence rested on continued successful performance in the private sector of the economy. Recruitment to that class was thus somewhat open for the most energetic and fortunate local families. Bureaucratic recruitment too had this "somewhat open" feature, which preserved acquired experience through limited rates of movement up and down the status ladder, but also provided for steady recruitment of the most energetic and ambitious. Further, the preservation of ties of mutual interest between bureaucrats and gentry tempered the ever-present tendencies for tax collectors to take excessive advantage of the coercive monopoly of the state.

A major reason for the successful maintenance of the regime was, no doubt, the challenge posed by the continuing threat to national security. Northern tribes constantly threatened or actually carried out invasions of China proper. The Chinese responded by building the Great Wall and by maintaining an army that was often the world's largest. This was a major reason for the empire-wide tax collection operation; it also gave the Chinese continual confirmation of the proposition that eternal vigilance is the price of security. When the Chinese lowered their guard, a time of invasions and other troubles ensued.

Chinese social structure was, of course, far from perfect. The monarchic system was, in China as elsewhere, a major internal cause of the periodic decline of Chinese life into a time of troubles. The period of Western contact in the nineteenth century coincided with such a period of decline, which accounts for much of the negative reaction of Westerners to what they saw there. The local economies were traditional in organization and resistant to change; this was no trading economy, and it was unable to withstand substantial penetration by the outside world in the nineteenth century. But the lessons it offers, summarized above, provide some fundamental support for contemporary conservative positions.

Venice in many ways seems the complete opposite of China.[2] A mere city state at the top end of the Adriatic Sea, whose population during a good part of her history ran to not much more than a hundred thousand souls, she was located for much of that time at the center of the maelstrom of Mediterranean and European politics. She was surrounded by much larger states—Hapsburg Austria, the French and Spanish, who used Italy as their principal battleground, and the Turks, not to mention the rival Italian city states, several of whom were much larger than Venice. Nevertheless, Venice survived for a millennium as an independent and unconquered state, for over half that time with substantially the same basic social structure. Not only is this durability a record for the time and region, but even in domestic affairs Venice seemed far less disturbed by conflict and class division than any of her contemporaries. Once again we have a society with a secret weapon.

During its half millennium and more of social stability, Venice was ruled by an oligarchy of some 200 families. The chief executive, the doge, was elected for life, but his children had no right to succession. In fact, the structures of the electoral system and the system of committees that bore legislative and executive power were designed expressly to prevent the doge from acquiring the ability to dominate political life. Even so, he was available as a leader with wide powers during times of great stress.

Two additional features stand out as part of the Venetian success story. The great families were mostly engaged in trade. A typical successful career pattern would have a son engage in a number of trading voyages and then settle down in Venice to help run the family business from there. He would begin to serve on some of the less powerful governmental committees and gradually move into more serious involvement in affairs of state, perhaps leaving business affairs largely to other close relatives. When he reached the pinnacle, becoming either doge or member of the Council of Ten, he was a man rich in knowledge of both Venetian and world affairs. He was already an experienced executive, and he would have no doubt at least some experience of war, the times being what they were. And basic decisions would be taken on the basis of the collective judgment of at least a dozen men as worldly as himself. No other state could match this skill and judgment, and Venice reproduced it generation after generation for centuries.

Nowhere was this skill more severely tested than in the effort to preserve Venice's independence in the face of surrounding predator states. The Venetians successfully combined a preference for peaceful trade with a willingness to fight with all their resources to preserve independence when necessary. Only relatively rarely did this continued high level of preparedness lead to attempts at conquest, and even then the act of conquest often had a strong element of defensiveness to it, as in her relatively late and modest expansion into the territory surrounding the island city.

Another and central point about Venetian affairs: She operated with a small bureaucracy. Clerks and secretaries were needed, men who knew the law and the details of the operation of the society's political system. But not many such were needed, it turned out, especially if the bureaucracy was to function as a genuine instrument of the will of the leaders and not become an autonomous and resource-devouring body. This was no doubt something the Venetian merchant-rulers had all learned before they took up the reins of government, and they kept the bureaucracy in check for centuries.

The small bureaucracy did not imply the absence of a welfare system, however. Venice was probably less subject to famine during its history than any other comparable territory in the region. The Venetian government had a grain board that provided for distribution of grain to residents during times of food shortage. This was an essential ingredient in their famine-control program. But equally essential was the market. The Venetians, with their unequalled economic intelligence system based on traders' and consuls' reports, were able to take advantage of the wide variation in grain prices in various parts of the Mediterranean as a normal part of their trading activity. When a bad crop year came to Venice and its normal suppliers, this intelligence was used to buy up the necessary grain at the best available prices. The system functioned so well that serious deprivation came to Venice perhaps only once over these centuries, while it must have occurred a dozen or more times in even the best organized of the other lands of the region. It was a low-cost and very effective system. Accompanying it was a model—for its time—and also low-budget public health system.

The centrality of the family in Venetian society is very striking. Family members tended to be involved in the family business, and family and state affairs were conducted on the assumption of the durability of families. Building for the next generation was obviously a major incentive for the participants. And, of course, the family served as a support, a social-security agency, for its members.

Elite circulation was quite low in Venice. In fact, for centuries only members of the 200 or so families whose names were inscribed in the Golden Book could hold significant political office. Adoption was a device that provided some upward mobility, but clearly that mobility was quite limited. Nevertheless, Venice thrived as did no other state, its leaders rising to the occasion time after time. Furthermore, domestic Venetian affairs seem to have been extremely tranquil. This was not a product of brutal exploitation; on this dimension too Venice ran a quite mild-mannered regime. There were opportunities for the lower classes too, in crafts and petty trade, for example. The general prosperity of Venice created opportunities that could never have existed in more democratic but less stable societies of the time. A worker, it seems, did not aspire to be doge; but he did aspire to obtain a higher income and to leave something for his children. In Venice energy devoted to economic activity could produce this result often enough to keep such people relatively satisfied.

Venice, of course, did finally decline, sinking into a half century or more of stagnation before succumbing without a fight to Napoleon's armies. But even this decline offers its lessons. A major factor in later Venetian history was the expansion of the bureaucracy into a large and corrupt spoils system. This occurred when opportunities for the poorer nobility to make money in trade declined. Tied to their aristocratic traditions and social structure, these young nobles were not allowed to follow the market signals regarding their relative economic worth and so sink into less well-paid occupations. Instead, bureaucratic sinecures were found for them. Competition for these jobs led to the sale of offices and the usual sad tale of developing malfunction. In addition, the enriched nobles finally followed the course of aristocrats elsewhere and moved out of trade and into landholding, turning much of the trading activity over to foreigners. Estates of those times being largely self-contained, the nobles lost interest in problems of the larger society. Deterioration of the bureaucracy through growth and the separation of political and economic power seem to tell the story of Venetian decline. For the "upstart" merchants were thriving in the eighteenth century; it was not that there were no longer opportunities, but that the heart of the Venetian system had been transformed.

China and Venice may well be the two greatest national success stories of prenineteenth-century history. Certainly their social structures were among the world's most durable, and the message they pass on to us is essentially a conservative one. One might put its essence into four propositions.

1. The primary basis for upward mobility (and downward too) should be economic performance, the creation of economic values.

2. Those who make the basic economic and political decisions in the society should have a self-managed stake in the successful functioning of the economy.

3. That state is governed best which is governed least.

4. Eternal vigilance is the price of national security.

The nineteenth century was to add a fifth proposition.

5. The most effective, dynamic, and stable economic system is based on the thoroughgoing market economy.

When properly interpreted, these propositions could stand as the basis of the conservative position; and each has been tested over the centuries in history's great success stories.

CHAPTER 4

England and the United States: The Thoroughgoing Market Economy

HISTORIANS usually place the start of the so-called Industrial Revolution at about two centuries ago. But having done this, they then point out that preparations for it were underway during the two centuries before that time and that the eighteenth-century changes came in at a modest pace. Then they add that this "revolution" is still in progress around the world. Some revolution! If they were all like that, you would never be able to tell a revolutionary from the rest of us.

A much more appropriate term for what has been going on has been suggested, namely, the Rise of Modern Industry.[1] *Modern industry* means production that requires relatively large amounts of fixed capital, such as factories and machinery and railroads and electric power stations. This emphasizes the single most important feature of modern economic times. And though, if you compare England today with England two centuries ago, "revolutionary" change has certainly occurred, that would not be the case for any two points in time that were, say, a decade or two apart. That is, there was quite steady change, so *rise* is also a more appropriate term.

The process was initiated and continued for reasons that have formed a central part of the conservative position. This should not be surprising, since important aspects of the conservatism developed as attempts to understand what was going on in this era, which posed important new problems for the individuals who were economically active. And though this new experience was largely a development of the eighteenth and nineteenth centuries, it has not lost its validity in the twentieth.

First, however, we must deal with the origins. How did it come about? It began, of course, in England, which in the eighteenth century was a great trading nation, with an economy that had considerable resemblance to that of the Venetian Republic, though writ on a larger scale. Merchants were already influential in government, and there was widespread recognition of the central role that trade played in generating the nation's prosperity. In fact, the increasing prosperity over the preceding century or two was a product of increasing trade, which of course is simply a question of merchants seeking out and finding profitable opportunities.

However, trade-based prosperity has its limits, unless increasing supplies of goods can be generated that can be profitably traded. Merchants were accumulating circulating capital, the money that was needed to buy the goods to be sold later. But this kind of investment was quickly turned over. Merchants tended to be leery of sinking their funds for long periods of time into an investment. The world seemed too uncertain a place for that. What caused them to change their minds? The answer to that question produces the key to the rise of modern industry.

Part of the answer lay in the consequences of previous success. Over time there had been a very substantial increase in the stock of circulating capital. This made the cost of money cheaper, lowered the interest rate, so that a potential factory builder found the costs of going into business cheapened. Furthermore, the richer merchants had become wealthy enough to be willing to take an occasional flyer on the more risky but potentially very profitable fixed-capital ventures.

This increased availability of capital created a favorable environment for the rise of modern industry, but could not generate the factories by itself. What had to be added was science, the systematic exploration of ways to harness nature to the satisfaction of human wants. The seventeenth-century science of Newton and others, combined with the technological development of the following century by such men as James Watt, created the technical opportunities that the economic environment made profitable. The conditions of both supply and demand had become extraordinarily favorable.

Probably the most important reason that these conditions had both become so favorable was that the institutional environment supported the developments. In the first place, there was the much-reduced impact of restrictive guild regulation as compared with the rest of Europe. For a century or more English mill owners who made use of water power had been escaping from the cities to the shores of more distant streams where the water flow permitted efficient use of water power to turn over the machines. In the countryside the guilds were relatively ineffective in controlling quantity, quality, and production methods, and of course the mill owners chose the lowest-cost methods. This is a very important factor, as can be seen from comparing the backwardness of the woolen mills, where guild regulation remained strong because mechanization came late, with the far more progressive cotton mills.

Second, there was the ability of the government to adjust successfully to new information. As the English cotton textile industry expanded by leaps and bounds, the government came to understand the institutional reasons for this success and to allow the guild regulation to die, or to abolish it. Thus additional industries were free to take advantage of the new freedom to follow the market's dictates, with similar consequences. This became vital even to cotton textiles in the early part of the nineteenth century when the advent of steam power led the industry to follow its profits nose back to the towns.

The government was flexible about these matters because it had already gone through an important adjustment in power relations.[2] The political upheavals of the seventeenth century had produced a kind of coalition and partial coalescing of the great merchant and land-owning families. The British ruling circles thus had an understanding of the needs of commerce built in, so that it was not so difficult as it was elsewhere to convince them as to what needed to be done. In fact, some of the needed steps had already been taken. Among the most famous was the ending of the Patents of Monopoly, which were simply sales of monopoly rights to individuals as a revenue-generating device for the crown; a new kind of patent was allowed, namely, the right of individuals to benefit privately from selling or licensing an invention. This latter was very important to James Watt, among others, in spreading rapidly, and profitably, the new steam engine that he had invented and teamed up with Boulton to produce.

A number of changes of the above kind were developing in England in the eighteenth and nineteenth centuries; they can be summarized by saying that private property rights were being developed and publicly recognized to an extent unprecedented in the rest of the world. This produced a tremendous burst of energy within the population. A potential entrepreneur could go into business with far more confidence than elsewhere that the government would not interfere with the operation of his firm, and indeed through the developing legal system would be prepared to defend his rights against the predatory. And scientist-inventors such as Watt had some assurance that they could reap a profit from the commercial success of their inventions. This sort of stabilizing of expectations could not but further support the other forces favorable to the introduction and expansion of modern industry.

The structure of government had yet another fundamental consequence, namely, the favorable environment it offered to the advance of science and technology. England was a leader in these areas far beyond her share of Europe's population. In general, science and technology flourished where freedom flourished, and England and Holland, the great trading societies of the time, were precisely the places where freedom and science flourished most freely. These societies were refuges for those who were fleeing from tyranny; but more, they were also pragmatic societies, where the connection between science and commerce was valued, where prizes for solutions to scientific and technical puzzles of practical significance were offered, as in the prize offered for the first person to provide a practical basis for estimating the longitude of ships at sea; and where colleges were founded that were oriented toward teaching and researching the "practical arts." This connection between the trading society and political freedoms, so notable a feature of past history, has, of course, survived the rise of modern industry and today distinguishes the modern trading society from its socialist counterpart.

All these factors came into play to set the process in motion. But then, acting in combination, they tended to trigger further developments that provided still more stimulus to modern business, gave England a still greater competitive edge in international trade, and consequently increased the pressure on other countries to follow England's lead. One of the main ways in which this worked led to the improved functioning of individual markets. For example, the capital market became a steadily more effective vehicle for mobilizing and allocating resources for investment. As the volume of investment increased, the various suppliers of capital found themselves increasingly aware of the same opportunities; this, of course, meant competition among them and tended to generate uniform prices for similar types of loans. And on the other side of the market, the entrepreneurs found that the prices of the goods they purchased tended increasingly to fall under the competitive pressures of markets and improved information. All this served to stabilize expectations and to create still more favorable conditions for further progress. At the same time, devices for mobilizing capital improved. Not only were banks able to shift savings from regions where there was a surplus to deficit areas, but new forms of business developed to make investment more attractive. Most notable was the limited-liability company, legalized in the mid-nineteenth century in Britain, which permitted the smaller investor to participate in a company's profits without committing all his resources to the paying off of potential debts of a failing company. The same forces were at work producing similar changes in other major markets, for land and labor, and for products as well. In all these cases what was happening was that property rights were being developed, particularly by enhancing the ability of the owner both to use his assets without unnecessary restriction and to sell or buy goods and services at will.

There was one final development that in effect was a codification and generalization of all the other changes. This was the development of a very close interconnection among markets, and the spread of markets into nearly every nook and cranny of economic activity. The businessman could evaluate costs with confidence because each item he was likely to need could be bought on a market at a price that was readily discernible. He could evaluate his revenue, actual and potential, with relative ease because the same was true of his products, or soon would be if it was a new one. The investor had a comparable improvement in his ability to appraise profitability, since profit is the offspring of revenue and cost. Information tended to spread rapidly about new developments as those who saw the opportunity competed eagerly to obtain funds from the market, and those with funds sought out new ways to put their money to work profitably. And, of course, all this activity was generating a rapid rise in the volume and kinds of goods produced, goods that would be of no use to these capitalists unless they could find people who wanted them and could afford to buy them.

This latter point brings us to the question as to how capitalism, the regime of modern industry, has dealt with the workers who had no capital but their labor to offer. The answer is well known to every honest economic historian: The nineteenth century saw a rapid and sustained rise in the real wages of the working classes. As the last paragraph suggests, this was no accident but was a factor strongly imbedded in the logic of the system. In nineteenth- as in twentieth-century capitalism the rich got richer, the middle class got richer, and the poor got richer. The thoroughgoing market economy emerged and functioned in an environment of general enrichment.

Not only standards of living rose. Freedom too expanded and developed throughout the nineteenth century in Britain. Step by step the vote was extended until all adults were participants in the political process. The level of education continually improved, as did the supply of books and of knowledge in general. Newspapers created a general public that was better informed about national and world affairs than ever before in history. And dissidence became institutionalized in political parties. The connections between the political and economic processes are obviously intimate, and British levels of freedom were only to be approached in other thoroughgoing market economies, most notably, of course, that of the United States.[3]

The American republic, like the Venetian republic, was not conceived by its founders as a one-man-one-vote affair. Rather, it represented a development of the basic Venetian idea, calling for both the urban middle class and the small farmer to have their voices heard in the councils of power. True, the voice of the small farmer was to be based on one-man-one-vote elections to the House of Representatives, but indirect election of senators and the president were expected to give special weight to urban commercial interests. The mechanism did not quite work out as planned but essentially the desired outcome was produced over much of American history. The principles on which this result was based were those of justice and order. Justice was promoted by giving each man the right to have his interests represented politically, and order by an electoral system that was capable of adjusting to changing power balances.[4]

With no aristocratic class and no entrenched guild system to oppose, resort to the market as the basic resource allocator was almost automatic. In principle, government was primarily concerned with providing a stable framework, and was kept small enough that practice could not deviate very substantially from the ideal. An ambitious young man would not think of going into government service as a means of furthering his ambitions. Productive economic activity would be what he sought. And this in turn led to the rapid expansion of farming and trade and, later on, of manufacturing.

Thus by a different route a firm basis was laid for the development of a thoroughgoing market economy in the United States. That condition was not achieved until the second half of the nineteenth century. The system of slavery in the Old South was one hindrance to that development though, as will be seen in chapter 6, market theory offers a somewhat different interpretation of the nature of that problem than is customary. However, another drag on the emergence of the thoroughgoing market economy in the United States was simply a product of the immense size of the country and the undeveloped nature of the transport system. Markets in different regions could not develop very complex interactions with one another, and so stabilize prices and expectations over the whole system, until the transport and communications base for a national market had been laid. Throughout the nineteenth century the United States was moving strongly in that direction. It might be noted that the government had a considerable involvement in many transport developments. It may have served to hasten progress, but the cost of federal government action of this kind can be partly measured in the contribution government made to the creation of great fortunes. Much the same thing could be said of the government's involvement in land markets, though government involvement in land ownership would have been harder to avoid under the peculiar conditions in which the country was founded and expanded its territory. At-least in this area the government organized a vast program of reducing its ownership of land, thus permitting market forces relatively free rein. The result was one of the most explosive episodes of economic growth and transformation known to history. The "minimal state" had proved its mettle.

In these two countries all the power of the five conservative principles mentioned at the end of the last chapter was demonstrated. The upper ranks of these societies came increasingly, in the United States overwhelmingly, to be occupied by men of experience with business, and their role in shaping government policy came to be increasingly important. The governments tended to be small—the American government's budget at the turn of the century was about 2 percent of the value of the national product, and Britain's, though relatively larger, was still miniscule by contemporary standards. The market had thoroughly penetrated every aspect of economic life. And they were free societies, the freest of their era, with a high level of domestic order.[5] The British, understanding the need for security, maintained the world's most powerful navy to provide for the island's protection.[6] The question to which we must now turn is whether this form of society can continue to function successfully in the changed conditions of the twentieth century.

CHAPTER 5

Markets and
the Twentieth Century

IN the twentieth century the economy has become much more complex. It is often argued that, as a consequence, the market does its job less well, the implication of course being that big government has been a badly needed development. However, there is no real theory to support this sort of conclusion. The theories of government that are popular these days in fact do the conservative job quite well: They point out the various ways in which government produces decisions of very poor quality. Essentially, the liberal line of argument does not use any theory of government at all. It first argues that the market cannot do the job well, and then assumes that the government, being a device to serve the people, will set everything to rights. Both theory and practice suggest that though the market is not perfect, it generally does a better job than government in delivering the desired goods.

For the moment let us concentrate on that nineteenth-twentieth century comparison. For example, some of the problems of market operation in the nineteenth century could be laid to the door of poor information flows. Problems of long communication time often led to goods continuing to be delivered to one market for some time after inventories in that market had begun to rise. It is even thought that a series of short-period business cycles in England may be attributable to the cumulative effects of communications time lag; for example, goods shipped home from India would keep piling up on British wharves for months after home demand had slackened off.[1] Letters written by hand take a long time to write, and often to read as well. Postal systems were rudimentary and in many places nonexistent. Hand delivery of messages about town was costly and time-consuming. As a consequence market decisions were often based on crude, partially informed guesses.

The reader, of course, can anticipate the twentieth-century response to all this. Typewriters, electronic data processing, radio and telephonic transmission—in a variety of fundamental ways the market has supported an incredible improvement in the speed and quality of information made available to the user. And where important problems remain, as with the postal service, the difficulties obviously are not the result of market failure; indeed at the present writing private delivery systems, such as United Parcel Service, are increasingly—and profitably—substituting for the inefficient government service. Once again, it is a market response that deals successfully with the problem, producing among other things the elimination of a whole genre of business cycles. Another thing to note is that this revolution in information if anything has improved the *relative* performance of markets vis-à-vis governments. Markets are organized to generate, process, and disseminate information of the kind and in the form that their users need; and markets are centrally concerned to keep this information flow in order. Government has a much more ambivalent attitude toward information. It wants the information in order to assist government decision making, but it does not much want the information to get out, where it might prove embarrassing; and those same motives exist for individual bureaucrats within the government. Combine this ambivalence with coercive power and you get the result noted in chapter 2, namely, bureaucracies that remain historical enigmas because they have managed to suppress so much information. Informationally speaking, they are the black holes of social space. Consequently, when there is a general improvement in information flow, much less of it will serve to improve government operation and much more of it will serve to improve market operation. Given the tremendous reduction in the cost of obtaining information, this has to represent a substantial improvement in the relative performance of market over bureaucracy in the twentieth century.[2]

There is no doubt that things have become a good deal more complex in the twentieth century. Deals tend to be bigger, the terms of contracts often contain literally thousands of clauses, and the time span of validity of contracts is often measured in years and tens of millions of dollars' worth of goods and services. What in fact has been the effect of this increasing complexity?

Accompanying it has been increasing creativity. There has been a scientific revolution coinciding with, perhaps even generating, the information revolution. The increase in scientific information has opened the door to creating new technologies; and at this point markets have come into their own as creative institutions. It is true that government has sponsored a large part of the scientific research—though it should also be noted that many of our leading universities, such as Harvard, MIT, Yale, and Chicago, are privately endowed. But it is under the pressure of market incentives that these technological possibilities have been transformed into effective realities. The comparison between Western market societies and bureaucratic socialism shows this in most striking form. The Soviet Union has a first-rate scientific establishment, fully aware of and even contributing to world scientific advance, at least when its Stalins are not instructing the scientists in their business. But despite massive efforts, the Soviets seem unable even to reproduce modern technology. In field after field, from commerical aviation to computers, from petroleum-industry equipment to chemical factories, the Soviets—and such once highly developed satellites as Czechoslovakia—must turn to the West if they are to get decent equipment to work with. Even in the space program, once supposed to be the shining example of socialism's superiority, we have recently been discovering just how crude the Soviet program was relative to the market-supplied American effort.

But the creativity of markets does not stop with the generation and commercial adaptation of technology. Organizational creativity has also been its hallmark. The structure of the modern corporation, and most strikingly the multinational, is certainly novel, and has grown out of the pressures of the marketplace to come up with an organizational form flexible enough to respond effectively to the massive new information flows, and effectively controllable under the constraints of the market environment within which it must operate. Once again socialism is either groping with crude marketlike forms of organization or attempting to emulate Western management practices, or both. The complexity of the developed twentieth-century economy has produced a variety of challenges to which the market system has clearly risen. And the secret of its success is a simple one, namely, the fact that material self-interest tends to be rewarded on the marketplace if it can generate goods and services that others want enough to be willing to give up the acquisition of other goods in order to be able to afford them. In a bureaucracy innovation is viewed with suspicion, since it is likely to be a threat to the authority of someone.

A third argument has it that the market system might be all right if it remained competitive, but that here is a built-in tendency for competitive markets to become monopolies. Consequently, government must step in either to preserve competition or to take over the operation of whole sectors of the economy.

The first and most important thing to notice about this line of argument is that the gross facts contradict it. A century or so ago there were undoubtedly far more monopolies in the United States, and probably in Britain as well, than there are today. For in those days the poor quality of the transportation system made it possible for local monopolies to abound. Especially if their products were heavy or bulky, these local monopolists were often able to extract the full monopoly price from their customers. But accompanying the information and scientific revolutions there has also been a transport revolution, which has turned these isolated markets into single markets national in scope. The result in most industries has been competition among a number of firms for the consumers' dollars and a substantial reduction in the number of monopolies.[3] During the twentieth century firms have grown, but so have markets, and by and large the one has canceled out the other.

A monopoly is defined as a single agent that has gained effective control over the total supply of some resource. If we simply take that definition and look around us in search of monopolies, our eyes will inevitably be drawn, not to the marketplace, where the monopoly is a rather rare bird nowadays, but to that biggest monopoly of all, the government. And the resource that government always legally controls the entire effective supply of is a very troubling one, namely the legitimate use of coercion. Coercion has historically been perhaps the most valuable of all resources, being the primary source of income for countless despots down through the centuries. There seems to be no alternative to concentrating its use in the hands of a monopoly, but it does throw a new light on much of the talk about monopoly. When agents of the biggest monopoly of all start talking about putting down capitalist monopolies, it sounds just a bit like using their own monopoly of coercion in order to squeeze out potential competition. This is not, of course, to claim that large private corporations lead blameless lives of public service. They are the instruments of people who are trying to get either rich or richer. But it *is* to suggest that one should always be suspicious of proposed controls that will have the effect of making the biggest and most threatening monopoly of all relatively bigger still; and one should be especially wary if the claimed goal is to reduce monopoly.

How did government come to be so overwhelmingly the dominant monopoly in American society? This certainly was not true of the nineteenth century. There are several points involved. First, there is a factor that can also serve as a sort of parable of our own time. One of the ways in which government became bigger was as a consequence of its involvement with railroad development in the West (that is, west of the Alleghenies). There was a tremendous potential market for the grain that could be produced on the endless plains, as well as for other products. But the investment required to run a railroad over such long distances was discouraging to private capital, and the profits in the medium run speculative, despite the golden longer-term prospects. Government was brought in and then used in ways that both rewarded promoters handsomely and fostered the development of monopolistic practices. Vast tracts of land were handed over to railroad companies, the roadbed grants covering a far wider swatch of land than was needed just for the railroad, while also serving as a firm base for monopolizing traffic. The attraction of this kind of operation, which involved a good deal of bribery of legislators among other things, tended to attract somewhat unsavory characters, who form a rather gaudy chapter in American history and founded some of the great American fortunes in the process.

So this joint business-government operation helped skew the income distribution as well as helping to generate some very strong monopolies. Over time the citizenry of the growing western states found these monopoly practices intolerable; they organized politically and eventually managed to impose a substantial level of regulation on the railroads. This had modest effects on railroad practices but helped make government still bigger and more powerful. Then when the railroads, gutted by those unsavory if government-favored financiers, went broke, government was brought in to help bail them out; after all, the citizenry wanted low prices, not suspension of service. And when rival modes of transportation developed, new schemes of regulation were cooked up to ensure "equitable" price structures, and the level of government involvement in the economy took a few more leaps forward. This process of interaction between economic problems and expanding government, together with mostly unneeded government aid, has continued for more than a century in this area of the economy, the latest episodes being the proposed government support for the mismanaged and bankrupt Penn Central Railroad and the government takeover and inefficient operation of railroad passenger service.[4]

The message is clear enough: Once government gets seriously involved in joint economic operations with private companies, the government role is likely to expand continually, since there will always be new opportunities for it to "help," whether by bailing out the victims of previous poor decision making or by serving as financial patsy for some new promotional venture. The appropriate line between government and business is the usual market line, and there is always a *prima facie* case against any proposal for the government to *give* a government service to some agent on the other side of that line. And, of course, that stricture does not apply only to *businessmen* who are seeking a handout.

The subject of creeping government encroachment immediately brings us to one of the most vociferous of liberal arguments. This is the claim that where there are externalities, the government must step in if good outcomes are to be generated. Externalities, which refer to "third-party" effects, or effects flowing from the implementation of a contract that fall on parties who are not a part of the deal, can be found most everywhere if one looks hard enough. So the argument for government involvement in almost every market is felt by liberals to have been established in principle. Clearly, if this line is accepted, there will soon be nothing but government operation of the economy.

Fortunately, it is not a very powerful argument. It has always been one-sided: The market is imperfect, therefore the government ought to do it. There is not any theory to show that government will do it better. But arguments to the effect that government will nearly always do it worse than the market are, in fact, quite powerful.[5] The problem facing a conservative today is in getting that message across. As will be indicated later, there are some grounds for optimism on this point, but there are also grounds for pessimism, based on the personal stake in government provision of certain services that so many individuals and businesses have today. The government has very powerful weapons in the service of buying support for a policy of government expansion.

These issues will be the subject of the next two chapters. For the present it is enough to note two things: once again the complexity and diversity of human wants and the creativity and adaptability of markets in the service of those aims; but also the unpredictability of humans, their tendency to whim and fashion as well as to wild outbursts of energy in the service of odd goals. Markets cannot be expected to deal at a very high level of effectiveness with such organisms, bureaucracies still less. But the point is, we don't really seek instruments for "dealing with" human behavior, only ways of living together that permit us to express ourselves freely while keeping the harmful effects on others within limits. A powerful and steadily growing agent who possesses a monopoly on the legal use of coercion is a very unlikely candidate for doing this successfully.

CHAPTER 6

Property Rights

IN RECENT YEARS a number of economists have begun to develop what amounts to a new field, namely, the economic analysis of property rights. Of course, the notion of property rights is an old one, and economists have written on the subject in the past. But much of this earlier work was flawed, mainly because the writers failed to appreciate the very close connection between the market and property rights.[1] We now turn to a description of the new approach together with a few examples of its application.

A private property right consists essentially of legal and social permission granted to an individual exclusively to use some resource, combined with permission to transfer that right to others. Of course, a private property right is only of interest if it is effective, that is, if the propertied individual does in fact have the ability to control the use and transfer of the resource. An individual's collection of property rights constitutes his room for independent maneuver in society, which of course relates closely both to his level of affluence and to his level of freedom.

If property rights are to be effective, they must have several key properties. Two of them, exclusivity and transferability, are mentioned in the definition in the last paragraph. In addition, a right must be well defined, so that both the owner and others know exactly what the owner does own. A right must be enforceable if it is to have any real meaning. And finally, the costs involved in defining, enforcing, and effectively transferring rights must be sufficiently low, relative to the value of the right, for owners to find it worthwhile to exercise their rights.[2]

The most obvious kind of property is real estate. In the United States today an owner has, more or less, the right to use the land himself and to sell it when and to whom he wishes. His rights in the property are defined at law and in the survey of the boundaries on file at the local land-registration office, and these rights are enforceable at law. There are, of course, costs involved in transferring the rights, and in enforcing them, but most of the time the costs are a small fraction of the value of the rights, as is evidenced by the frequency of exercise of the right of sale.

Though real estate probably represents the most typical kind of property, in fact anything that can become the subject of a deal can be viewed as property in exactly the same way. One can even have a property right to a service—for example, by signing a contract with a company to clean your office every week for the next year. Of course, in practice there are some legal restrictions on the property rights of the owners of almost all kinds of property, and property-rights analysis centers around the justification—and particularly the lack of justification for many—of these restrictions.

We will be discussing property rights in more detail in this and the next few chapters. Right now, an example or two will serve to indicate the great importance of property rights in defining an individual's economic situation and his opportunities for improvement. Consider first a farmer on a medieval manor. He and his family would be assigned the right to cultivate a tiny plot of land in some larger field, which was divided up among the other villagers. But this right was restricted in a number of ways. Every other year his land would have to lie fallow, the fences torn down and village cattle free to graze on his plot. The small size of the plot and its propinquity to neighbors meant that the timing of plowing, planting, and harvesting would all have to be controlled by joint decision, or by decision of the bailiff of the estate. So, in fact, the farmer could do very little individually to improve the productivity of his own land. He could not even sell the rights that he possessed, if he wanted to leave for town. The fact that he did not have an exclusive right to the use of the land was a serious brake on progress, and indeed the manorial economy was an especially backward one. Real progress only came after this form of holding had been abolished.

This example has some contemporary relevance, for in most socialist economies something very much like the manorial form of agricultural organization has been recreated. The peasants—the word farmer is not appropriate for such serflike creatures—are bound to the soil in this variant of socialism; that is, they are not allowed to leave the "collective" without legal permission. They are compelled legally to put in so many days a year of work on the collective farmlands. Their rewards, however, are miniscule, as is suggested by the fact that in the Soviet Union about a quarter of all agricultural output is produced on roughly the one twentieth of the land that peasants are allowed to work individually. One could hardly imagine a clearer demonstration of the inhibiting effects of the lack of an exclusive property right on incentives. Nor is there likely to be a clearer demonstration of the peasants' own view of this most common form of socialism, the collective farm, than their response to an offer to abandon the collectives and return to private agriculture. This occurred in Poland in 1956 and in Yugoslavia two or three years earlier. In both cases over 90 percent of the collectivized peasantry immediately redivided the land and returned to their former "bourgeois" ways. One last point, which relates to the rationale for such a system: When the Nazis conquered the Soviet grainbelt province of the Ukraine in World War II, they took one look at the collective farm system and decided to retain it. Their leaders could think of no better system for extracting a maximum of the harvest from the peasantry at minimum cost to themselves.[3] Who in his right mind, when comparing the life of a private farmer with these beasts of burden, would call the *former* the exploited ones?

A precise definition of any particular property right is obviously important, since it would be difficult to either use or sell your property if you are not sure just what it is you have in your possession. A patent law, which gives the holder sole right to the use, licensing, and sale of the benefits from an invention for some period of time, is an example of a property right that has been defined by state action. Without that definition the inventor has lost most of his material incentive to invent. But, perhaps as important, he may also have lost access to resources that would make the act of invention possible. Once the right is defined, those with money may be willing to subsidize certain kinds of innovative activity. The modern university is a case in point, where patents for the innovative work generated in its laboratories are, by agreement with the researchers, assigned to the university.

But it is important not to exaggerate the role of the state in defining property rights. Usually the key steps are taken in the marketplace. For example, patent law could only be contemplated after it had become widely recognized that innovative activity was often profitable, and further that it was in the general social interest to support such activity. Recognition of these two points requires a fairly sophisticated knowledge of how societies work. That knowledge was to come from business activity. Once again it was the businessman who, far more than others, had the appropriate experiences for developing the relevant understanding. Only in the Middle Ages in the West, and much later—if ever—elsewhere, did this recognition spread far enough to produce effective property-rights definitions for inventions. Not surprisingly, it was in commerce-oriented Britain that the key steps were first taken. And, of course, it was not just a matter of the businessman's experience, but the greater frequency of innovation in the more open environment of the commercial society that contributed to this outcome.[4]

Clearly, if property rights are not enforced, they are not worth much. And equally clearly, there is a role for government in the enforcement of property rights. However, once again it is important to realize that by far the major enforcement activity is generated by the private sector itself. Historically, for example, the Law Merchant, which governed relations between traders at the great medieval fairs, grew up out of merchant practice and was enforced by the merchants themselves. And today in the United States enforcement of property rights as defined in business contracts is, by a factor of more than ten to one, done privately and outside the judicial system. What typically happens is that the contract itself calls for submission of disputes to arbitration. Private arbitrators who are knowledgeable in the practices of particular trades are organized to provide this service for a fee. The merchant who loses such a private arbitration award has a powerful incentive to accept the decision, for otherwise his credit as a reliable businessman will suffer. And, of course, resort to the law remains as an option if the merchant feels strongly enough about the issue to bear the costs and uncertainties of legal action.[5] Throughout a market society one will have no difficulty in picking out the many other ways in which private activity dominates the enforcement of property rights.

There is one more point that is relevant in understanding the basic idea of property rights, namely, the cost of establishing them. In some cases it may simply be more trouble than it is worth to try to define and enforce some property right, in which case the right will tend to disappear. A rather striking recent example of this occurs in the older sections of some American cities. Buildings in these areas have been subject to a large variety of regulations, such as rent control, permission granted tenants to withhold rent on the basis of alleged building code violations, increasing complexity of building code rules, combined with increases in the cost of compliance, and restrictions on the right of eviction for nonpayment of rent. In many cases the landlord finds it no longer profitable to assert his property right in the building; he simply abandons it. This happens because he is no longer at all clear as to just what his property rights in the building are, and in addition he finds the cost of enforcing what rights he may have prohibitive. Interventions in the market system, which were the product of well-meaning but economically misinformed politicians and interest groups, thus ended up producing a decline in both the quantity and the quality of housing available to the poor.[6]

Having defined the concept of property rights, it is now time to point to some of the ways in which it can be used to gain insight into the fundamental issues of our day. We may begin with that basic socialist notion, enforced sharing. Many are attracted to this idea, especially when it is given more attractive names, such as "solidarity" or "commune." But in practice what it always turns out to be is enforced sharing. Even so, one might ask, surely there *is* something attractive about the idea of working together for a common goal and sharing the fruits of that labor. Indeed there is. The problem is not in that basic aim, one of the noblest of human aims. The problem lies in the particular method of implementation. When individuals are put into groups and told that their reward will be proportionate to the output of the group as a whole, the individual has lost most of his incentive to produce. The difficulty lies in the fact that he has lost his exclusive right to the fruits of his own labor.

This loss of incentive accounts for much of the lower productivity evidenced in both agriculture and industry in socialist countries. But often such collaborative effort is unavoidable. Factories in capitalist countries are often large, and involve hundreds of people operating in teams. How do they manage to attain higher efficiency levels than their socialist counterparts? The answer lies in the right to offer or withhold the use of the services they command, a right that each individual possesses in a market economy. In this case the laborer has alternative sources of employment, and the factory owner has alternative sources of labor. Performance must meet market standards or an alternative will be found for the worker. And the employer must meet market conditions of labor and reward or alternative employment will be found by the worker. The Chinese commune member and many of the more valuable and highly skilled employees of socialist factories typically do not have this opportunity, or the incentive of market competition. The lack of exclusivity and the lack of ability to transfer the resource, two key aspects of property rights, are defective or absent; the result: inefficiency and unpleasant conditions of work.

But what about that noble aim of working together and sharing the fruits of labor? The answer is that a regime of property rights, a market-based economy, is precisely the one that gives the greatest stimulus to such activity. No system of sharing is worth much unless the participants are there by their own choice; and in the long run it will not be worth much unless there *are* fruits to share. But those are the things the regime of property facilitates. Knowing what the various parts of a package will cost and will be worth, because the market prices tell them; free to enter into voluntary agreements with confidence that their property rights are protected, the participants in a market society tend to be on the lookout for just such opportunities of mutual labor for mutual benefit. The difference is in the voluntary nature of the agreement, the concern of each that he will receive a sufficiently large share of the fruits that it will justify his participation, and free to leave if things don't work out to his satisfaction: This is the sort of arrangement for cooperative work that the market generates. This is the essence of a capitalist enterprise. If results are any criterion, it is superior in every way to other arrangements, which by definition involve in some form or another coercion of the participants.

A description of the role of capital in society offers another opportunity to show the fundamental role of property rights in generating an affluent and orderly society. In Marx's view the problems of capitalism all stemmed from the monopoly of the means of production, the factories and farms that are the tools for generating output, which the capitalist class possessed. We have seen that something very much like monopoly of this kind did exist in Venice, and that it played a role in the ultimate decline of that city-state. And in nineteenth-century England it was certainly true that a relatively small number of people owned the factories, and most of the farmland too.

But that is not a monopoly. Ownership of *all* scarce resources is restricted; that is precisely what scarcity means. And no one would say that everyone ought to own a factory, for that would be an impossibly inefficient drain on our scarce resources. A monopoly occurs when *one* agent owns or controls the means of production. And only one kind of society fits that bill, namely, the socialism that Marx and his followers want to replace capitalism with. In a sense Marx's prediction has been vindicated; in socialism there is monopoly ownership of the means of production by a tiny ruling class acting in concert as the Communist party; but the results are pretty awful.

In a market economy the regime of property rights implies the very opposite of Marx's charge. The market provides access to the means of production for all who can afford to participate. And participation does not require great wealth. There are over 15 million private individuals in the United States who own shares of stock. And there are millions of capitalists who exert direct control over the means of production as owners and managers of small businesses and corporations. This occurs because the market is a voluntary mechanism, because it stimulates incentives to work and hence generates more affluence than other forms, and because it generates efficient use of the means of production since each potential use of capital must compete with others on the marketplace. It is the openness and competitiveness of the process by which capital is generated and allocated among competing uses that is the essence of capitalism. In fact, the power of these processes is illustrated by the Venetian case. Given the size of the economy, restriction of control over the means of production to some 200 families turned out to be sufficient to keep these voluntary, competitive pressures at a high pitch. Over a period of centuries these pressures dominated the distorting force of restrictionism and permitted Venice to function successfully. Some concentration of wealth actually serves to stimulate progress by increasing the supply of funds available to be put into expanding future production, as our exemplary market economies show all too clearly.

Many other examples of the role of property rights in the economy could be cited, from the development of credit to the control of pollution. Some of them will be discussed as we go along. But enough has perhaps been said at this point to establish that property rights are an essential feature of a successful market economy. Their relation to the processes of government is the subject to which we now turn.

CHAPTER 7

Government and Property

GOVERNMENT and the bureaucrat are inseparable. The latter is the fellow who operates the former, not as an elected official responsive to the needs of his constituents but as a cog in a large and complex machine. No one has much good to say about the bureaucrat, and with reason. However, there *is* one nice thing that can be said about him, and we will begin the discussion of government and property with that remark.

The bureaucrat is a human being, not different in any essential way from the rest of us. His problem is that he is put down in an environment where, behaving in a quite human way, he produces horrendous results. It cannot be a very satisfactory way of life, so eliminating as many bureaucratic jobs as possible will release both his victims and the bureaucrat himself from misery.

The problem of the bureaucrat stems from the nature of his job. A typical bureaucrat is assigned some clientele, say, applicants for food stamps or for a small business loan or for a hunting license or for a particular routing of a new highway. In all likelihood he hasn't chosen his clientele, and they certainly haven't chosen him. Second, the bureaucrat's success or failure depends not nearly so much on whether he satisfies his clientele as whether he satisfies his boss. Just what his boss wants varies from situation to situation, but, human being that he is, the boss bureaucrat typically wants a minimum of trouble. He doesn't want a lot of complaints to handle and he doesn't want to have to make a lot of tricky decisions. If there is a difficulty, bureaucrat and boss bureaucrat want to protect themselves; so as a matter of routine anything out of the ordinary will be passed up the line as far as possible for decision. The possibly devastating effect on the client is of little interest to the bureaucrat; or at least there is no way the client can make it worth the bureaucrat's while to take him more seriously without violating the laws against bribery. Actually, there is one way, namely, by exerting influence at the top of the hierarchy to get special treatment. This works quite well provided you have that kind of friends, but the result is clear enough: The bureaucracy will give little consideration to special need but will give careful consideration to the especially influential.

Finally, there is a property of the government bureaucrat that has the effect of turning the merely frustrating into the rather sinister. The government bureaucrat represents the agency that has been assigned a monopoly in the application of legalized coercion in the society. Behind the bureaucrat stands that vast panoply of process servers, inquisitors, and jails that, in a very direct way, legitimize the bureaucrat's unconcern. The bureaucrat will always want information before he acts, and the rational—but uninfluential—citizen will always feel just a touch of the fear inspired by the awful majesty of the state as he considers his responses and where they may lead.

The market is a means of getting jobs done superior to bureaucracy in each of these dimensions. The market is a voluntary mechanism—no cops lurking in the background to go into action if you say no deal. The businessman's assistants have a much more clearcut incentive to please the client, namely, if it brings in profits it makes the boss happy. Furthermore the firm—and this applies to nearly all of them in the United States—will not be a monopoly and so has a direct incentive to satisfy the customer in order to retain the business. There is no alternative government to go to for your licenses and subsidies.

Of course, the market isn't perfect, and there are some jobs it does not do too well, such as actually managing the national defense. But all we are arguing is that there should be a very strong case for letting the market do the job, given the problem of the bureaucrat, before resort to government is made. And this bias against government control of economic activities has been a central part of the conservative tradition, as earlier chapters have suggested.

Unfortunately, the matter cannot rest there, because there is built into bureaucratic government an almost irresistible tendency to grow, which tends to make a mockery of even the best intentioned conservative governments. One might remember that in Ronald Reagan's tenure as governor of California the state budget doubled. The same tendency toward growth has been observed in other conservative administrations at both state and federal levels, both in America and in Britain.

By now it is well known that this tendency toward growth is built into bureaucracies. Parkinson's famous law tells us that in a bureaucracy the number of tasks assumed tends to rise to the level of employment. And Niskanen's analysis of bureaucracies has shown how much of their behavior can be explained simply by assuming the bureaucrat is trying to maximize his budget.[1] That, of course, is quite a plausible assumption, given that the influence of a bureaucrat tends to be measured by the size of the organization he heads.

Once again the comparison with the market is instructive. The businessman too is often judged by the size of the operation he controls. But the difference is that his operation is tied far more closely than the bureaucrat's to providing services his clientele actually wants. And the size of his organization is measured in terms that reflect this level of service, namely, sales and cost, including the rate of return on the capital supplied to the business. The bureaucrat's operation will be based on only one of these, cost, for the value of his service will not be measured in a marketplace and so cannot be measured in terms of price. Move to a big new building and double your staff and you have become a much bigger success, almost regardless of the effect on the level of service provided. This is the secret of empire building in Washington and the other centers of government around the world.

Just as these lines are being written, a whole new giant bureaucracy, the Department of Energy, whose employment will run into the tens of thousands, is moving into its big new headquarters in Washington; there is a good deal of talk of a Department of Education; my state's budget, under two reputedly penny-pinching governors, Ronald Reagan and Jerry Brown, has tripled; and my home town, whose population has risen less than 20 percent in the past two decades, has just taken over two good-sized buildings to house our expanded city staff. It seems there are many successful bureaucrats these days.

Before turning to the question of how to control bureaucracies, the connection between big government, that is, big bureaucracies, and property rights needs to be pointed out. Actually, the problem is the lack of connection, for the existence of bureaucracy usually implies that important infringements of property rights are occurring. In the first place, where there is big government property rights will tend to be relatively ill-defined. This stems from the uncertainty as to just what decision a bureaucrat will render, a decision that may determine whether you have the legal right to start a business or receive some other benefit that only the bureaucracy can bestow. The uncertainty, of course, is a consequence of the situation of the bureaucrat, discussed above, and especially of the lack of mutuality in the relation between bureaucrat and client.

Second, bureaucracies have often been brought into existence for the express purpose of infringing or eliminating many existing rights. They are created to restrict your right to drive your truck on certain roads, to compel the installation of various so-called safety and anti-pollution devices, to make tax rulings that substantially increase your liability in various ways, to enforce licensing requirements that increase costs to many and deprive some of their livelihood; and so on ad infinitum. Much of this power is the product of what is known in the trade as "discretionary authority" and, given the complexity of the regulations under which the bureaucracy will almost certainly be operating, the authority that results can be very great.

Big government often creates serious problems of enforcing even those property rights it has defined and recognized because of overlapping jurisdictions among agencies; for example, the enforcing agency may be independent of the agency that confirms the right and may be unwilling to act. This sort of buck passing is familiar to everyone who has had dealings with a bureaucracy. And then too there is the tremendous increase in the cost of preserving one's property rights in the face of all these harassments. Even though success in fighting the bureaucracy may be attainable, it may not be worth the victim's time and money.

Finally, and possibly most important of all, there is a massive creation of what might be called public property rights. Each bureaucrat has his own little sphere of influence, which consists in the right to make decisions one way or another over some restricted range of problems. The bigger government gets, the greater the likelihood that any particular private property right will come into conflict with one of these bureaucrat's rights. Where does the injured individual go for redress? The answer, of course, is that he must go to government, and all too likely to the offending bureaucrat's boss. One can hardly expect justice to be done when the judge is an interested party. The Watergate events provide a long list of situations of this kind. And so the larger the government, the more massive the infringements of property rights.[2]

This is quite a depressing picture, a picture of a government that performs poorly but continually expands. Where can one look for help in bringing it under control? One place one might look is the electoral process and the legislature. In a democracy, if the people want to reduce the bureaucracy they elect legislators who are committed to doing just that, and the problem is solved, right?

Unfortunately, the correct answer is wrong. For generations now scholars have been trying to produce an analysis of democracy that shows how well it functions. But no one, however erudite or sophisticated, has managed to improve on the old saw to the effect that democratic government seems like an absolutely abysmal form—until you look at the alternatives. It wins by default, not because of its "optimality properties."

One major difficulty in the present context has to do with the relation between majority rule and property rights. If a majority can change the law at will, all property rights that are protected by the law are in constant jeopardy. And for any particular property right, it is usually not too difficult to put together a majority vote against it, since property rights can usually be categorized in such a way that only a minority holds any one of them. Nor are individuals at their best when deciding the fate of others, as opposed to their own. For all these reasons, among others, majority rule is capable of producing some very bad outcomes.

The American founding fathers were well aware of this fact, being keen students of the classical democracies—and of the history of Venice, it might be noted. Their notion was that the majority should be represented but should not rule absolutely. The system of checks and balances was designed explicitly with a view to curbing the power of the majority. The dual system of legislatures, followed at the federal level as well as in many states—which has been threatened by the recent misguided one-man-one-vote decrees of the courts—was one of the keys to their system. What this means is that the legislature represents a variety of interests. What it is supposed to produce is not an ideal outcome but a workable compromise among these interests.

Unfortunately, government has become one of the most important of those interests. Legislators can influence bureaucrats, all right, but the reverse is also true, the bureaucrats' weapons as always being harassment and delay in dealing with one's opponents and open-handedness in dealing with one's friends in Congress. Even the president often finds that if his program is being stalled in the bureaucracy he is more able to get what he wants by creating a new agency than by attempting to reform the existing agency against the opposition of the many influential friends it has carefully nurtured. That is probably an important part of the reason for the creation of the Department of Energy, and it leads to the confident prediction, based on past history, that most schemes of governmental reorganization will achieve little. And to both legislature and presidency there is the constant pressure from potential beneficiaries to provide more services. So it appears that the electoral system cannot be relied upon simply to take the will of the majority and act upon it.

Among the most interesting of recent cases of this kind of influence has to do with the Nixon proposal for providing a guaranteed minimum income to the poor. A major reason for the failure of the proposal to pass Congress was that the government "service" bureaucrats opposed the measure. And why did they oppose it? Because it bypassed them, threatening their jobs by substituting money for the administrative "services" they provide.[3]

The Law vs. the Bureaucracy

The importance of the law, from the conservative point of view, is shown by the fact that it arose as a means for adjudicating conflict involving those two basic institutions, the family and the market. Near Eastern and particularly Roman law first emerged as family law, as a set of rules for dealing with conflicts between families, particularly where some harm had been done by one family's members to those of another, leading probably to breaches of the peace if society did not impose some solution. And much of contemporary law dealing with property rights is an evolving product of the medieval—and ancient—Law Merchant, a set of rules administered at first by the merchants themselves, as noted earlier. As times have changed and societies have grown more complex, the law has changed too. Today it represents the codified experience of a hundred generations.

If markets were the place where the basis of property rights was first laid in the act of exchange of goods, it was in the law that the concept and institution of property rights was given explicit form. Rules for determining ownership and obligation were worked out as a consequence of experience that provided a firm and defensible basis for trade, and one that would not be cluttered with excessive litigation and conflict. And as experience accumulated and society changed, the rules accumulated and changed too. In Anglo-American common law this process is highly visible in the process of making and adjusting precedents in the courts. But it is present too in the civil-code countries of the European continent, where the codes have undergone a very similar process of evolution in response to similar social developments. Law has thus developed everywhere in the West into a major source of wisdom with respect to dealing with practical problems of human conflict.

One must bear in mind, of course, that by "the law" we mean a good deal more than a set of books containing all that wisdom. The court system with its judges and lawyers and—in America, at least—adversary proceedings are essential to it, as are the investigating and enforcing arms of the law, the prosecutors' offices and the police. But even the judiciary taken as a whole is minute in size as compared to the executive branch. In 1965 the federal judiciary had a total employment of 6,000, compared with 2.5 million civilians in the executive branch. It is also highly decentralized, with great care being taken to prevent encroachment by one jurisdiction on another. The judiciary is obviously a very different animal from a bureaucracy.

And this brings us to a major conservative principle, which is especially valuable in the struggle against big government: In thinking of reform the effort should be oriented toward making the system look more like the judiciary and less like the executive branch. And along with this will also go the rule: Keep it simple! A governmental apparatus restructured in accordance with these two rules has some fundamental advantages over the present state of affairs. In the first place, it is clear that such a government would have far greater respect for property rights than is possible in a bureaucracy-ridden environment. For the stock-in-trade of the law is to determine the rights of the parties and to make a judgment on the basis of what rights have been infringed.

Second, the cost of administering such a system should be a fraction of the cost of bureaucratic intervention. The law is structured to respond to conflict situations and to attempt to resolve the conflict in a way that will be both just and efficient, which means less likely to cause more conflict in the future. And the law tends to be oriented toward creating an environment within which people work out their problems on their own, again in sharp contrast with the bureaucrat's direct and active involvement in the affair.

And finally, the judiciary functions as the mirror image of the ever-expanding bureaucracy. The legal system works better the less the resort to it. A good law is one that is just, is widely understood, and whose enforcement is something everyone can reasonably expect. Under such circumstances violation of the law is likely to be infrequent. The same applies to infringement of property rights; if they are reasonable, are well defined, and enforcement is expected, they too are unlikely to be infringed. And judges have little incentive to expand their workloads, in striking contrast to the attitude toward his agency's "workload" of the ambitious bureaucrat.

Now, of course, the law is a far from perfect institution. There is such a thing as a bad law, not to mention a bad judge or an ill-trained policeman. The judiciary is a human institution. It has a number of advantages over bureaucracies, among others that because of its long tradition it tends less frequently to ask its members to do ridiculous or impossible things. But it does go astray. When that happens one is likely to note an increase in litigation in the area at issue, because when the law does go astray it is usually because of problems with definition or enforcement of property rights. But at least that provides a public sign of a problem, again in sharp contrast to the bureaucracy's tendency to keep all its dirty linen carefully concealed from the public eye.

The next two chapters will be largely devoted to offering examples of how these two principles can be applied to problems of contemporary government. In closing this chapter we suggest one classic case that illustrates the principles enunciated above in a rather pure form. The case involves federal regulation of radio broadcasts.[4]

Regulation of radio broadcasts grew out of a genuine problem. When commercial broadcasting began in the 1920s, any broadcaster was free to transmit on whatever band he chose with a transmitter of whatever power he chose. The result was a great deal of mutual interference and conflict. After considering a variety of alternative forms of control, including nationalization of the industry under the Department of the Navy, a system of regulation was established that involved the licensing of broadcasters. When the latter met the requirements set up by the new agency, now called the Federal Communications Commission, it was assigned a wavelength and permission to use it for a period of years until the license expired. As the years went by, the regulations became more detailed and all-embracing, including substantial control of the general pattern of programming and even the content of specific broadcasts. Several stations have been denied a renewal of their license because of specific programs they have broadcast. And as the years went by, of course, the agency not only expanded its competence to regulate in a variety of directions but also expanded its staff continuously—for example, in the ten relatively quiet years of regulatory activity between 1955 and 1965, the commission's staff increased by 50 percent. The typical pattern of bureaucratic operation was being followed to a T—except for the fact that the commission's programming controls are probably unconstitutional, a violation of the First Amendment right of free speech.

Now consider the judiciarylike alternative to bureaucracy. The first thing to note is that the problem that generated the initial legislation is a serious one, affecting national defense as well as private communications in a vital way. However, the basic problem is actually a very simple one, namely, a lack of definition of property rights in broadcast frequencies. New technology does not always generate a clearcut property right, and such was the case here. Supposing then

that the government served as the definer, and enforcer, of such rights.
A simple and effective scheme would require only that the government
serve as registrar of the rights. In this case it could treat the frequencies much as it treated the billion and more acres of public land
that have passed through its hands in the last two centuries. That is,
instead of leasing broadcast rights, it could sell them outright and enforce the property right of the purchaser. Bands could be reserved
for national defense, but an even more effective outcome might be to
require the armed forces to obtain their wavelengths in the same way as
private users, thus providing Congress and the public with a clear
picture of the cost of this aspect of national defense. The advantage of
the latter approach is that undoubtedly the armed forces would not retain the 90 percent of the wavelengths they now hold, thus substantially
lowering the cost of using the airwaves to communicate.

Suppose such a system were introduced. How would it differ
from the present arrangement? Clearly, it would take very little government activity; after the initial sale there might be occasional subse-
quent sales as new technology opened up the possibility of using additional frequencies. But aside from that very modest effort, about all
that would be needed would be a register of ownership of the various
frequencies at various locations. Any problems would be a matter for
the judiciary.

There is no apparent reason why telecasts could not be handled in
exactly the same way. This is a strong case and the result is very
striking: a probable reduction in regulatory cost to perhaps 1 percent
of its current level. And there may be even greater opportunities in some
other areas, because in the broadcast example there actually is *some*
need for government action. So the final message of this chapter can
be an optimistic one: By using the property-rights approach and applying the principles of keeping it simple and using judiciarylike rather
than bureaucracylike forms of organization, the government leviathan
may yet be brought under control.[5]

CHAPTER 8

Government and Spending

THE most controversial area of government spending in recent years has been the welfare program. It is a massive program, involving annual expenditures far in excess of the defense budget, and it has been growing far more rapidly than the latter for a great many years. It is also a tremendously complex operation, containing literally hundreds of substantial programs aimed, at least so it is claimed, at alleviating or—as many would say—eliminating poverty in the United States. And no one seems to be able to stop the growth.

Naturally, this gigantic mess cannot be completely disentangled in a single stroke. But it is possible to point out some frequently ignored aspects of the mess and its causes, and it turns out that the suggested cures all seem to point in the same direction. The basic mistake has been the attempt to bypass the market in areas where it can do the job perfectly well, either by itself or with a minimum of definitional and enforcement assistance from the state.

A good place to start is medical care. American per capita expenditures on health care are the largest in the world but, judging from statistics, America has far from the world's healthiest population. As one would expect, the poorer sectors of the population have the highest incidence of ill health. The liberal response to this situation has been to propose massive new programs designed to get the government involved in creating a "health-delivery system" to the poor. Examples of nationalized health systems such as those in Britain and communist China are held up as shining examples of how to do this job.

At the moment the Chinese health system, with its barefoot doctors and acupuncture, is all the rage. What never seems to be noticed is that without any revolutionary fanfare a comparable system has been in operation in noncommunist China for decades. In Hong Kong and Taiwan there are modern hospitals with a full panoply of modern doctors and methods. But side by side with this there is "traditional" Chinese medicine strongly based on herbalist cures, and distributed widely over the poorer areas of these places. There is an element of quackery to some of this traditional medicine, but what medical system is wholly free of that? Many diseases are effectively cured by traditional medicine, and there is a growing interaction with at least some modern practices.

The thing that needs to be noted about the "secondary health-delivery system," as it would be called among government policy-makers, is that it is a low-cost system. The herbalists are paid fees that semiskilled workers and peasants in Taiwan and Hong Kong can afford to pay, when they themselves feel the need for the care. And these fees cover the costs of the supply of the service, so problems of overuse and of haggling over fair prices do not absorb the time and energies of large bureaucracies. And the results are suggested by the fact that the health of these populations appears to be comparable to that of the mainland Chinese. The communists' barefoot doctors program may be a success too; but essentially it is a mimicking of a system generated and sustained without political fanfare by the market systems of the "other" Chinas.

The moral for the United States is clear enough. Our problem is that government licensing of medical practice has, as in nearly all other government licensing systems, been effectively turned over to the licensees, in this case the doctors, to administer. And they, as would anyone following his self-interest, have arranged things so that the standard of medical care that passes their requirements is millionaire-type care. In effect, every doctor becomes a Park Avenue doctor because the government is guaranteeing Park Avenue prices for the supply of medical services. The recent expansion of government subsidies has expanded the demand for this kind of medical service tremendously, thereby increasing medical prices far more rapidly than the volume of medical services. And, of course, those who get left out tend to be the poor.

The solution is to make it possible for the market to supply inexpensive medical services to those who have less to spend. We even have a considerable body of people who with little or no additional training would be well equipped to provide many of these services, namely, nurses and former armed services medical corpsmen. What many people need to understand is that this does not mean that the poor will get poor-quality service. Rather, it means that they will not get the frills unless they want to pay for them. Much medical service is dispensed for cosmetic or psychological reasons rather than to create or preserve the basic health of the body. And much diagnosis and treatment is very simple, requiring nothing like the tremendous knowledge and skill of a current M.D. The place to sort these things out is not in Washington but on the marketplace. And that will not be possible until the government stops granting to the medical profession as a property right a de facto monopoly on the supply of medical services.

The response to past suggestions that the government stop licensing doctors compulsorily has been that it will destroy the quality of medical care, leading to the entry of a lot of charlatans into the health-care field. People who argue this way have not noticed two things. First, there are already a lot of charlatans supplying health care, as even a casual reading of the daily papers will reveal. But second, and more important, is the fact that the government does not now control quality in the medical profession. The government simply granted the monopoly right to doctors; having done that, it leaves the administration of licensing essentially up to the profession itself, acting through its chief organizations, such as the American Medical Association. If the government were to cancel its monopoly, the AMA would still have a strong incentive to make sure that everyone knew that people licensed by it are reliable, high-quality practitioners; indeed, if anything its incentive in this direction would be enhanced, for then there would be quality competition so that the quality price-differential that their members' services could command would be at stake. Then the road would be opened for the entry of lower-priced medical services. These too would no doubt develop their own quality-control organization and make efforts to see that the public understood that such quality control was there to back up their service. And, of course, the usual market informational mechanisms would be at work. Once this step was taken, one of the major problems in health care would be solved, while at the same time current government expenditures in this area would be reduced by a large fraction.[1]

Food, clothing, shelter, and health: These are life's necessities, a minimum supply of which are essential for the normal functioning of the human being. In successfully functioning societies some effort is made to supply these services to those in great need. The most successful, such as the durable and conservative societies of Venice and imperial China, had such programs, and they seem to have contributed substantially to domestic peace and stability. In the United States we have these programs too, but they seem to have had the very opposite effect. They have not even done a particularly good job of supplying the services, while costs have become astronomical, something over three thousand dollars a year per person on the most generous estimate of the number of poor, and probably in fact nearer twice that figure.

Why the great discrepancy? The answer is the liberal approach to welfare. Liberals have attempted to use the program to accomplish too many objectives, from income equalization to providing minority employment, from turning the poor into politicians to redesigning urban environments. Most of these objectives are resisted by large segments of the population, because their own interests are hurt in the process, and the diversion of resources to these various purposes has meant that relatively little money reaches the poor. A number of these objectives have to do not only with controversial matters but with goals no one even knows how to achieve. Consequently, the programs all leave a massive trail of ill-defined and poorly enforced property rights behind them. The inevitable, and, for a conservative easily predictable, result is inefficient supply of services and a substantial increase in the level of conflict.[2]

A conservative welfare program would not be operated at zero level, but it would be limited to serving the basic aim, namely, to make possible a relatively secure supply of basic goods and services to those in great need, and to do it at minimum cost. The medical example points out the great possibilities that exist for cost reduction by such devices as simply getting the government out of the business of granting monopolies. This approach also has great promise in the housing field, where much regulation is aimed far more at preserving the monopoly power of the building-trades unions than it is at promoting safe and efficiently built homes. We will not go into this area in detail, but one point might be worth making. Even if changes in property rights in this area merely lowered the cost of middle-class housing (it would in fact do far more than that), this would be of considerable help to the welfare program. For it would lead a number of families to move up to middle-class housing, thus in turn improving the quality and quantity of the housing available to the poor. And since the middle class is far more numerous than the poor, the relative increase in housing from any such shift would be greater for the poor than for the middle class. Once again we have an elementary point in the theory of supply and demand that is largely ignored in the current welfare program.

Of course, there are always limits to cost reduction. We are talking about scarce goods and their social cost can never be brought down to zero. Current programs are often aimed at bringing their private cost down to zero, at providing "free" medical service and the like. But the taxpayers have to pay if the recipient does not, and the overuse that such an approach generates means much higher costs, which in turn leads to big control agencies and the usual process of creeping bureaucratism. If the program is to be efficient, an attempt should be made to bring private and social costs into equality. That sounds like a subtle goal, and it would be, were it not for the fact that that is just what markets do. Marketizing the welfare program is therefore a central aspect of conservative policy.

And so we come to the final step in eliminating the welfare mess, the famous negative income tax. There is no need to nationalize the health services or to engage in massive public housing ventures. Indeed, as experience shows, there is every reason not to do that. Once normal—meaning dynamic and creative—market forces are again allowed to work in these areas, there will be a supply of services at a fraction of current costs. The income support required to make these services available to the poor would be correspondingly lower and, of course, the cost of administering such a program a tiny fraction of current costs.

One final point about the welfare program is, namely, the nature of the social obligation and the nature of the goals that can reasonably be achieved. In the first place, it is important to bear in mind that the poor will always be with us. It's a simple matter of definition. A very important aspect of poverty is *relative* lack of goods. It has been noted that as average incomes in the United States have risen, questionnaires asking people how much is needed these days just to get by produce answers that rise at about the same rate. Poverty in this sense begins at about half the current average income. The poverty war seems to go along with this in practice, with the obvious result that an anti-poverty program has to get bigger every year, and the more affluent we become the more the program will require.[3]

This is obvious nonsense. The government has an obligation, as most conservatives would concede, to eliminate any serious risk that Americans do not have access to enough of those basic goods and services to survive. And that is the end of it; to get more than the minimum of necessities is a matter of the individual's own behavior. Markets—and families and private charities—exist to deal with this situation. The markets work for those who have the willingness and capacity to produce things of value to others. Those who can find no way to get above the minimum by using these agencies may be objects of pity but not of general social obligation. The history of any welfare program designed to do more than this will bear a considerable resemblance to the recent history of the American welfare program, for it is bound to have monopoly and creeping bureaucratism and corruption built into it.

Of course, there are certain aspects of the welfare and other spending programs that we have not taken into account. For example, there probably is a place for government in certain areas of more direct action. One that particularly comes to mind is transactions costs, one of the major problems in some areas of market behavior that produces less than satisfactory results, as noted in the last chapter. The government can sometimes use its powers effectively to improve market functioning by reducing the private transactions costs. A good deal of the legislation designed to be enforced through the judicial system is of this kind, such as the laws regarding sales of goods. And, of course, the more privatized welfare system outlined above involves just such a shift in emphasis, from executive agencies to the judicial system. The individual's problems with the welfare system are then more likely to be ones that he will take to court than ones he will take to some social worker for resolution.

But the poor individual may not be aware of his rights and opportunities under such a system; certainly he will not just after it is installed. In such a situation it is a legitimate function of government to engage in a substantial informational program. This might even go as far as to provide some subsidized legal counsel during the transition period. But such activities should not be continued if there is any prospect of the service being supplied on the private market. And, of course, what this suggests is a reform of the monopoly power possessed by the legal profession in ways that correspond with the above medical revision.

There are many other areas of government activity that require substantial revision if an effective conservative policy format is to be achieved. But, aside from the question of economic stabilization, to be taken up in the next chapter, these areas, from education to agriculture, require the introduction of no new principles. Equipped with the already suggested ideas and the relevant facts, there is no great difficulty in working out the basic lines of revision needed. For Keep it simple! is one of those conservative principles.

CHAPTER 9

Money and Taxes

THERE IS a close connection between economic fluctuations and property rights. Upward and downward surges in the level of economic activity create unpredictable changes, often quite substantial ones, in the market values of various assets. This destroys some of many individuals' command over resources, and thus some of their rights to exclusive use and transfer of resources. Furthermore, the uncertainty generated tends to make transactions more costly as individuals must take additional time and effort in order to study the prospective volatility in the value of the assets they are thinking of acquiring. Even the costs of enforcing contracts are affected, because economic fluctuations continually generate unexpected outcomes, which often are not anticipated in the contract negotiations and so lead to conflict between the contracting parties. Clearly, property rights would be stabilized and their transfer made cheaper and more effective if economic stability could be achieved.

Unfortunately, nobody knows how to do it. Recessions, in the sense of a slowing down and occasional actual downturn in the level of economic activity, seem to be here to stay. This statement would have been highly controversial only a decade ago when the Keynesians and the economic planners were in their heyday. Today it is a no more than commonplace remark. This change in economists' attitudes was brought about by that most effective of all teachers of economics, experience. In the hope that this lesson once learned will not be forgotten, it will be useful to look very briefly at just what went wrong.

Planning is a word that Americans were far more suspicious of than most Europeans. But without actually using the word, the American government begin doing much the same thing that the West Europeans were calling planning. They began adapting government policies to serve the interests of economic stabilization, as those interests were interpreted by Keynesian theorists. Keynesian economists have been rather like that other well-known breed of technicians, the Dow theorists of stock-market fluctuations. Both have an esoteric line of talk based on assumptions that are not always apparent but when displayed seem to fly in the face of common sense. For the Keynesian the key notion, that of the multiplier, is based on assumptions about variations in the rate at which the economy's spenders will turn over money are in about the same class, as far as realism is concerned, as the Dow theories of breakthroughs and bases.[1] More fundamentally, the two theories are alike in trying to predict the unpredictable. It is a very common type of human endeavor and wherever it happens it leads to much the same kind of rococo elaboration of qualifications to every statement, as anyone who has looked at "systems" for playing the horses or beating the roulette wheel will know. Keynesian economics remains alive by staying at least one level of complication ahead of the facts.

But, of course, this did not stop the planners. Having made their case plausible to many and, more important, offering liberal politicians just the formula they wanted, economic planning was given its head. The formula required the government to be a big spender in the economy, or otherwise it could not be used to compensate for the presumed inadequacies of the private sector. There had to be a large government debt or it would not be possible to exercise enough influence over the capital markets. Then, once big government and big debt were achieved, fine tuning could begin. After a careful Keynesian analysis of the economic situation, the Keynesians believed that a program of corrections by government taxing and spending could be orchestrated with many other instruments of lesser importance to keep the economy on its "long-run growth path" except for quite trivial deviations. For over a decade in the United States, and for much longer in a number of other countries, this sort of policy program has been in effect; and at the present writing these countries have also been in a state of economic and financial volatility for a decade and have lived through the worst recession in forty years.

What went wrong? Part of the problem was an underestimation of the importance of monetary as opposed to fiscal policy. The Keynesians have never developed a plausible or workable theory of the relationship between real and money variables, that is, between theories explaining the financial side of the economy in its impact on the production side. Another part of the problem was political. Unless the economy were simply turned over to the experts to manage, policy measures involving a change in the level of taxing or spending had to obtain congressional and presidential approval. This often could not be obtained until after the policy had become obsolete even by Keynesian standards. Fortunately, the politicians were never sufficiently sold on the theory to be willing to turn the economy over. And part of the problem had to do with time lags built into the economy. Increased government spending, of course, is supposed to stimulate the economy. But different government spending programs require different patterns of spending, and these in turn filter through to other sectors of the economy at different rates. And individual receivers of additional money behave in different ways at different times. Particularly when decisions relating to the future—saving and investment—are at issue, the behavior is impossible to predict with any kind of accuracy, and the time lags between government stimulus and private response change from one situation to another.[2]

Often these problems, in a situation of intermittent ups and downs, produce effects that are substantially worse than doing nothing. An attempt to stimulate the economy gets its response only after the economy is on a swift upward movement, so the government policy creates not prosperity but inflation; and vice versa. It turns out that this kind of well-intentioned mismanagement was a major, perhaps the most important, factor in turning the recession that began in 1929–30 into the Great Depression of the thirties.[3] And already the chairman of the Federal Reserve Board has been castigated in the press for much the same thing in connection with our most recent recession.

What can be done to clear up this mess? Fortunately, there is an answer. It is not a panacea but it holds promise of substantial improvement. The answer involves concentrating far more on monetary than on fiscal policy in stabilizing the economy; hence it is compatible with the government-spending reforms discussed previously. Second, it involves substantially reducing the discretionary authority of monetary and fiscal policymakers. The fiscal policy measures would be substantially limited to the so-called automatic stabilizers: such things as unemployment compensation, which automatically but only partially compensate for a falling off in demand. And monetary policy in turn would be substantially limited to keeping the average growth rate of the money supply at some target figure. This in itself would be mildly stimulating to the economy. Once expectations—that the rule would be followed—were stabilized much of the threat of inflation would vanish. Thus a feature of this approach is that it meets yet another conservative rule for government, namely, Keep it simple!

Recessions will not be eliminated by such a policy, but they should be mitigated; and the policy can be defended without making claims to knowledge about how the economy works that do not exist. It is essentially a defensive strategy, and is in that sense conservative. It is in the private sector and among private individuals following their own chosen pursuits that one should look for creativity. When you get it from government policymakers, armed with their powers of coercion, it is rather frightening.

One other remark about recessions: They aren't all bad. Essentially, a recession is a time of reckoning for the overly optimistic, a time of cost cutting, a time of reestablishing a base in realism as a precondition for further progress. In a society in which the unfortunate victims of the recession are guaranteed the minimum basics of life, it is not too heavy a price to pay for this kind of readjustment. Schumpeter called it a period of "creative destruction."

Varying the tax rate is one of the standard "tools" in the Keynesian "toolkit." However, there is a good argument for throwing this tool away, aside from objections to the theory itself; namely, that its variation is a serious infringement of property rights. Uncertainty as to just what sort of exclusive rights you have to the use and control of your own resources is increased by government action. Given the partly unproven and partly false nature of the theory, the case against using taxes in this way seems decisive.

Once again as these lines are written we are being given a demonstration of the harmful effects of even a proposal for tax reform on the economy. President Carter campaigned on the issue, despite the fact that a tax "reform" had just been completed by Congress the year before. All during his first year in office uncertainties as to who would be affected and by how much clearly had a negative effect on private investment, which has failed to recover the way it has after previous recessions. Of course, other factors, such as uncertainty over new government environmental controls, also have played their role. The reform has just (January 1978) turned into a typical election-year tax-reduction showpiece, and uncertainty over its size and impact no doubt will linger for a few months more.

It is essential that taxation not destroy incentives; if it does do so, it will be by preventing an individual from enjoying the benefits of additional increments in income. In our present system a number of those in top-salary brackets pay nearly confiscatory tax rates; marginal rates in some states—California is one—reach seventy cents on the dollar. But what mostly happens is that the attempts to impose such heavy rates produce great ingenuity in finding legal ways around the burden. Ingenuity is a scarce resource and consequently expensive, and so the tax system ties up the time and energy of a great many of our most productive citizens. And the upshot is a system that becomes highly discriminatory, taxing some people very heavily while others escape taxes almost entirely.

But there is another and less well-known aspect of the tax system that is perhaps even more incentive-destroying in its effects. This is its action, in combination with the welfare system, on a large segment of the poor. A number of programs come together on people in the working-poor category. The net effect of these programs is to produce an effective marginal tax rate for a great many of these people that is very high, at times exceeding 100 percent. In other words, they would have to pay money if they want the privilege of working harder.

Once again the villain of the piece is complexity. A simple definition of income, a fixed rate above the minimum standard exemption, and a limit to permissible government spending based on the rate of economic growth, comprise the simplest possible tax system. It would not dramatically change the average pattern of actual payments; it would affect many of those singled out for special reward and punishment in the current system. It would save tremendous amounts of time and energy, perhaps most important of all. And it would define the nature of property rights in the economy far more precisely. And finally, a "welfare system" that consisted essentially in marginal subsidies ("negative taxes") to the lowest income classes would show up merely as a complication of the income tax law.

Another feature of current tax methods is worth a comment. The family, as already argued, is the most important generator of social cohesion in society, and the place where much of the quality of the next generation is determined. It is also the focus of one of the most powerful of human incentives—the urge to found a dynasty, to leave one's descendants in a more favorable situation. This institution and the energies it engenders should be fostered, not harassed. Liberals often talk as if they would prefer to eliminate inheritance entirely. But they seem to have missed these central points. An amusing aspect of the McGovern campaign of a few years ago was the senator's dramatic backtrack on the inheritance tax question when he discovered from the public opinion polls that most working-class people believe that a person of substantial means should have the right to transmit his property to his heirs.

But once again the tax system already has set up enough obstacles to inheritance to put hordes of tax and estate lawyers to work. And once again simplicity and the avoidance of confiscation and its close relatives are the answer.

No doubt many people feel that a program similar to the above does justice to the individuals concerned but would be harmful to society, because it would lead to wealth becoming concentrated in a very few hands. The feeling seems to be widespread that there is a natural tendency for markets to turn into monopoly, for wealth to become steadily more concentrated, and for government to be the only savior. We have already noted the irony of a policy that takes from the less powerful to give to the agency that is already by far the *most* powerful as the means for achieving a greater dispersion of power. But there is another, more direct argument, namely, that the available statistics do not support these claims. On the whole, industry has not been becoming more concentrated during the twentieth century. And the upper or richer tail of the income distribution shows something of a tendency to follow Pareto's law. This law says, roughly, that those who have get, absolutely but not relatively, and that throughout the upper tail of the income distribution the probability of a person, say, doubling his income in some time period is about the same regardless of his current level of income. This proposition is by no means proven, but it is in better shape empirically than any theory that claims that wealth is all flowing increasingly into a very few hands.

Once again Venice offers strong and reassuring evidence. Venice was a substantially less mobile society than our own, especially at the top where the state protected the leading families from the competition of others. Venice became wealthy and remained so for centuries as a result of producing and trading on markets, of using the market system. Taxation was low, except in times of war, and was not relatively burdensome on the rich. Nevertheless, over the centuries of the great merchants' activities, the wealth in Venice did not concentrate. People became far wealthier absolutely at the top, in the middle, and even toward the bottom of the income distribution. The evidence that we have suggests that in a dynamic market economy where private property rights are respected, well defined, and enforced, there is no reason to fear that an excessive concentration of wealth will develop.[4]

CHAPTER 10

The Problem of Order

ORDER is obviously an essential ingredient in the successful functioning of a society or an economy. If there is too much disorder,
the individual loses his ability to influence his own destiny. For the
understanding of conservative economic ideas, the most relevant kinds
of disorder are the product of assaults on person and property; that
is, they consist of the arbitrary and substantial infringement of civil
and property rights.

A discussion of order must be careful to distinguish between the
kinds of order. For example, a liberal would probably initially refuse
to discuss the issue of order at all. But if you persuade him that this
is a serious problem, he would no doubt try to tie order to the distribution of income. The liberal would argue that if there is not a fair distribution of income, there is bound to be social unrest. As will be
argued later, this is the very opposite of the truth. At the moment it only
need be pointed out that there is a close connection between order
and relatively stable expectations. If the citizens are reasonably confident that their property rights will be respected in the future, the
fundamental basis for order has been established. So there is a close
connection between order and monetary stability, the topic of the last
chapter. Once again apparently very different aspects of the conservative position turn out to be mutually compatible and even mutually
reinforcing.

A liberal response to this might well be: Of course, stabilizing
expectations is a good thing, and I advocate a policy of price fixing
so that, say, interest group X will not have to suffer the consequences of a higher price for their favorite consumer good Y. But this
misses the point completely. In the first place, there is the rather
obvious fact that periods of price control have historically occurred
principally during times of relative unrest, as the history of incomes
policies in Europe and in the United States in recent years attests.
Second, there is a good reason why this should be so. Price fixing is
an infringement of property rights, on the right of an individual freely
to transfer ownership of an asset. Inevitably it is done by the state to

protect a favored interest group against "the market," that is, against those citizens who own the asset whose price is to be fixed. This coercive intervention in the structure of property rights is inevitably resented, the favored group thinks it has acquired the "right" to unlimited access to the good at a favorable price, and the stage is* set for conflict. The more of that sort of thing there is in a society, the *less* secure expectations regarding property rights become, and so in the long run the more disorder you must ultimately endure.

The essential distinction is between human interactions in which there is a commonalty of ends and those in which there is, or need be, only a commonalty of means. Market exchanges are of the latter kind. You and I may both benefit from a mutual exchange of goods and services even though I disapprove of your motives in making the trade or your plans for the use of the proceeds. A great many market exchanges have this property, and the affirmation of rights and the rule of law is designed to protect such interactions. Such exchanges are means-connected but not ends-connected social interactions. When the state gets deeply involved with the economy, as with economic planning or extensive price fixing, it is intervening in these exchanges and imposing an ends-connectedness that can in time destroy the basis of a free society. It is thus fundamental to recognize the limits to which the state must be held in the pursuit of order.[1]

However, this is not to assert that there are no ends-connected transactions in society or that there is no role for the state in regulating them. On the contrary, the regulation, under a rule of law, of the appropriate set of ends-connected human interactions represents the primary and essential task of the state. We can perhaps best get some sense of how this works by looking at three of the most fundamental problems that societies have had to face historically and considering the appropriate ways that have been developed to regulate them. In doing so one should remember a somewhat different and more restricted notion of disorder than was used above. A situation tends to foster disorder when an increasing number of people find themselves facing a major dilemma, namely, a conflict between deeply held moral imperatives. At such times the structure of a society is in some danger of fracture or even collapse. When possible such situations should be avoided; if they cannot be avoided, some way effectively to control them must be found.

Religious wars and the persecution of people for their religious beliefs have played a major role in the history of the West. Hardly a country, hardly a religion has escaped this tragedy, and the misery and loss of life entailed is literally uncountable. However, over the last two centuries the incidence of religious persecutions in Europe and America has declined dramatically. And this in turn is obviously connected with the strong trend toward disestablishing religions. How is this result related to the means for creating a society of order?

The answer seems to go something like this. By imposing a commonalty of ends-connected transactions on a religiously diverse population, the state forced much of its citizenry to face a deep conflict between moral imperatives. The law-abiding believer in an unofficial religion was the individual who faced this dilemma most acutely. However, many enforcers of the law faced a comparable dilemma, for they could see the unpleasant consequences both of enforcing the law and of failing to enforce it. Disestablishment of the official religion did not, of course, resolve all problems of order that were related to religion. For example, the issue of abortion today is for many a religious issue, and it is certainly one of the major contemporary problems for state policy in the United States. Disestablishment did not eliminate all religion-related issues. However, it did serve to defuse them somewhat by making it possible to take the issues one at a time. Instead of a web of closely related ends-connected transactions that more or less as a unit created challenges to the social order, there is one or a few issues, each of which can be treated separately. The depth of the moral dilemma was much reduced. And often the remaining issues could be further defused by disestablishing the issue, so to speak. For example, in the case of abortion, eliminating direct government subsidy of abortion without prohibiting it to those whose moral scruples are differently engaged by the issue is one way of disestablishing a vital dimension of the dispute. Naturally, this is not the appropriate place to propose a solution to this problem; we are merely attempting to illustrate one method by which a major source of disorder can be dealt with by simply removing responsibility for regulating a realm of behavior from the sphere of state competence.

However, not all problems of "moral-dilemma" disorder can be dealt with effectively by simply removing the state from the activity. The central issue of the American Civil War exemplifies another type of problem. Here the state itself is faced with the moral dilemma. Either the civil rights of the slaves continue to be violated or the property rights of the slaveowners will be violated. A believer in freedom can have only one option in this case, and a believer in the rule of law has no way out but to extensively and systematically violate rights, either civil or property. Or is that really the only option? Consider the following hypothetical policy. The government announces the elimination of slavery within its boundaries ten years hence. At any time during that ten years a slave may buy his or her freedom or an owner may sell the slave to the government, in either case at the market price current on the first day of the offer. Any slaves remaining in bondage at the end of ten years are automatically freed without compensation. Funds for the government to purchase all offered slaves are to be raised by general taxation on the whole population of the country, including the slave population (which is to say, their masters).

This is, of course, a purely hypothetical case and no implications as to feasibility at any time before the Civil War are being asserted. It might be noted, however, that something like this was done in Cuba at about the time of our Civil War, though the conditions of barracks slavery there and the absence of an effective market-pricing system were serious weaknesses in that program and produced unfortunate results. But our point is that once the nature of the problem is properly posed—in this case a fundamental conflict among rights—it may very well turn out that there are acceptable compromise proposals that avoid shifting heavy burdens on special groups in the population and so in effect encouraging desperate responses. It might also be noted that freeing the slaves in an orderly manner and without a devastating war might have produced a much different environment for the slaves to begin their lives as free human beings. The fact that the government would have to determine the market price by administrative action rather than by the simple test of what the market would bear would lead to some coercion and some windfalls to some of the parties. This is no panacea. But one important feature should be noted, namely, the fact that such a scheme could probably only be designed by someone with some experience with the operation of markets. Once again it would seem that leaders of government who have such experience are relatively more likely to be able to deal effectively with this class of problems. And once again this particular trait goes a long way toward explaining the extraordinary condition of domestic order that existed during most of the long history of the Venetian Republic.

In our own times, one of the most fundamental issues is that of revolution. The typical socialist view of revolution is that it is the culminating act of a period of intensifying class warfare in an environment in which almost every political issue is a specific manifestation of that class warfare. Of course, the resolution of conflicting rights is a matter of no interest to socialists, who obviously favor a policy of generating public disorder as a precondition to their seizure of state power. However, the first thing to note is how wildly exaggerated the notion of class warfare is in the socialist literature. In fact, no revolution has been the product of the lower class rising up in righteous indignation over the unfairness of the distribution of wealth in society and casting out the upper class as part of their policy to redistribute the wealth in their own favor. Almost everywhere one finds that the working class feels that considerable inequality is perfectly justified. Far from viewing themselves as the victims of brutal oppression, they tend to be a mainstay of patriotism who find the general division of societies into many groups of unequal wealth quite reasonable. One remembers that the Republican party has traditionally derived a large fraction of its support from this same working class, and that working-class conservatism has forced the shelving of many a liberal and radical proposal of the Democrats, among them the McGovern inheritance tax mentioned above.

Nevertheless, revolutions do occur. Why? The answer is that revolutions have occurred only in situations in which the ruling class in that society has become unable or unwilling to govern. This is as true of the Russian revolution as it is of the Chinese revolution, as true of the Cuban as of the Angolan. One form or another of malaise, often corruption or gratuitous brutality, has served to destroy the legitimacy of the rulers. But at any rate, the one fixed factor in revolutions is the weakness of the regime. The typical revolutions of the twentieth century have been ones in which the revolutionaries are relatively few in number and weak, and have the support of only a small fraction of the working class. This is not surprising in view of the fact that the leaderships of revolutions have come not from the working class but from the middle or even upper classes, which somewhat weakens their claims to represent the downtrodden. So the problem of class warfare is a pseudo-problem, one not at all likely to occur, judging from the history of the past century. And the problem of revolution becomes a problem of maintaining a government capable of taking the basic steps needed to preserve order.[2]

However, an important qualification must be made to the above conclusion. Generally speaking, class warfare will not develop unless the government creates it. And, unfortunately, liberal governments have been busy doing just that in recent decades. One of the most obvious of such steps has been the granting of patents of monopoly to labor unions. In the United States unions are encouraged to form industry-wide organizations, they are exempt from antitrust laws if they do so, and a government body has been created, the National Labor Relations Board (NLRB), with wide powers to arbitrate, that is, to coercively decide on matters of dispute between union and business. This procedure seems deliberately designed to create powerful institutions representing a particular class and then to pit them against institutions representing the other class. One must admit that class warfare becomes much more plausible as an outcome after something like this has been going on for a while. In Britain similar developments may have already approached the crisis point. And, unfortunately, the story does not stop with unions but represents a general policy of liberal government. Great efforts have been made in recent years to establish organizations of the "poor" to create another dimension of class warfare. The government actually created the organizations and provided funds for the leaders so that they could bring some clout with them to city hall. This particular aspect of the "war on poverty" was fairly quickly aborted as a result of prompt action by mayors and local governments in a number of cities. But many programs with similar impact remain.

The message here is simple enough. Neither revolution nor class war is a natural procedure or attitude for the working class in contemporary society. Where it occurs it is the product either of a failure of will on the part of the leadership of the society or of its deliberate creation by liberal politicians. That is to say, once one understands it, this problem should not be too difficult to eliminate.

There is one other kind of disorder that is, this time with good reason, much on the mind these days. Crime, the infringement of rights by individuals and small groups acting deliberately to further their own interests, has become a problem of rapidly increasing moment.[3] Record rates of increase in crime are recorded year after year. People who twenty years ago did not even know anyone who had been victimized now have direct experience. Training and equipping the police force, adding computerized information systems and the like, seem to have no effect on the rates. It is as if some new epidemic illness had broken out and spread rapidly among the population.

The metaphor is not a bad one, though not everyone will appreciate it. For the metaphorical sickness that is referred to is not intended to represent the mind of the criminal. The problem, perhaps the central problem in understanding crime in America, has to do with the liberal response to it. When the question of crime comes up, the liberal responds that here is an area where he, for once, is prepared to start by emphasizing the need to protect rights against violation. Unfortunately, what he is referring to is the rights of the criminal. It is true that criminals, as citizens, have the right to a fair trial, and that that right should be protected. However, liberal actions have gone far beyond this, including extremely lenient sentencing, plea bargaining, second and third chances even for repeat offenders who have committed violent crime, and so on. Among the most striking has been the expanded use of the insanity plea, which has returned dangerous criminals to the streets with clocklike regularity. Having achieved this dramatic reduction in the rates of punishment for crime, liberals have turned to the prosecution and trial processes with similar results, so that it is now substantially more difficult to obtain a conviction than it was in the past. Most recently liberals have been at work on prisons, their efforts being devoted to making the place look more like home.

Most crime seems to be committed by people who see an opportunity to benefit materially from depriving others of their rights. Thus one would expect that, other things equal, if there is an increase in the opportunity successfully to obtain goods by theft, the crime rate for theft would increase. Basically, that is the phenomenon we have been observing in the years since the liberals have gotten effective control of the criminal justice system. Having made the expected gain from criminal activity greater by reducing the risk and cost of being punished, a large number of people have been recruited to the ranks of the criminals. Of course, that is not the whole story. Our society is more affluent now than it was twenty years ago and the mere presence of more goods tends to increase the opportunity. It is also true that the number of juveniles has increased and, no doubt due to their attitude toward risk, a disproportionate share of crime is committed by this age group. But these last two factors cannot explain the magnitude of the increase in crime. Permeating the whole environment has been the liberal notion that says in effect that the rights of criminals are to take precedence over the rights of victims.

But liberals too are victimized by crime. How then can they think as they do? It should be remembered that liberals tend to be fairly affluent and are likely to have been leaders in the move to the suburbs, so the incidence of their victimization by crime is probably much lower than for the population as a whole. It might also be noted that liberal attitudes with respect to this problem have been undergoing some changes recently as crime has come to touch the lives of all of us. But basically the liberal attitude toward crime seems to have had another root. Once again liberals have been caught trying to use crime policy in order to implement a goal that was almost entirely unrelated to the criminal justice system. That aim was the redistribution of wealth and income. Their goal of an "egalitarian" society has been pursued wherever they could find a lever that would seem to take from the rich and give to the poor. And as it turned out, once one understands the goal, making crime easier is one of the great liberal success stories. There is little doubt that liberal policies toward crime have made a large number of poor criminals substantially richer!

The appropriate measures to turn this appalling situation around seem to speak for themselves. Serious or repeated violations of the civil and property rights of others should bring the culprit into contact with a swiftly and sternly acting criminal justice system. Rules of evidence and procedure should be fair, but they must be consistent with speedy trial and sentencing. Punishment should be fairly precisely specified so that deterrence is clearly established. It should be recognized that no rehabilitation scheme has much chance so long as crime pays. Consequently, punishment should be substantially devoted to keeping obvious criminals off the streets. Evidence from other countries indicates clearly that all these things can be done without violating the accused's rights to due process. Of course, not all the effort should be devoted to the system of criminal justice. Opportunity has another dimension as well, namely, the ease of access to the desired objects. But this side of the problem of crime is not essentially a government responsibility. Citizens who leave the keys in their cars and the doors of their homes unlocked are contributing to the crime rate as well. Clearly, as crime rates have increased, citizens' interest in protecting their own goods has increased *pari passu*. What is needed now is to recognize that criminals too respond to these "price" signals in their behavior.

The problem of order is one of the central ones in any society. It is not a problem for which there are easy answers. One always feels a little reluctant to advocate the use of coercion. But the basic message *is* simple. A government that is unwilling to use force in the service of order creates far more violence through growing disorder than it does by serious efforts at deterring revolution, crime, and other rights violations. A government that has the reputation for swift, sure punishment for established rights violations will have far less need to use violence. After arming their government with those two principles, members of a society can reasonably expect to live out their lives under conditions of domestic order.

CHAPTER 11

Economic Development

THE SAME conservative principles apply to developing as to developed countries. Liberty is a basic desideratum and is threatened by concentrations of power, whether in the economy or the polity. The special problems of developing countries stem largely from the vagueness with which property rights are defined and the uncertainties associated with the enforcement of property rights. In addition to this, there is a strong tendency in many developing societies, especially socialist ones, for institutions to be manipulated so as to create substantial divergence between private and social costs and values, so that the economy keeps getting pointed in the wrong direction. Once these ideas are understood, issues relating to economic development and to socialism become clear enough.

The conservative position on economic development probably creates more skepticism among readers than any other topic. The misery and corruption and brutality that seem to be so much a part of the developing world have led even many conservatives to despair of the validity of their principles for these countries. But advocacy of the principles is not just a matter of defending untested abstractions. There are, in fact, a number of countries that have been successfully applying some basic conservative principles to their economic development. A brief calling of the roll is thus in order.

Socialists these days start with China, and so shall we. The rate of growth of industry in Taiwan over the past two decades is substantially higher than in mainland China.[1] Agricultural development, preceded by a land reform that made freehold peasants of most farm families, was rapid in the first decade or so of Taiwanese growth, until Taiwan had become a substantial net food exporter, a status mainland China is still far from achieving. The health status of the population is good, perhaps as good as that of the mainland population. There has been no foreign economic aid during the past decade or so. Taiwan has developed using the basic capitalist instruments of markets, foreign investment, and government stimulus without overwhelming government involvement in economic activity; consequently, the prospective entrepreneur can reasonably expect that gains achieved in the market-place will not be sucked off in large and indeterminate amounts by a corrupt bureaucracy.

Very similar stories can be told for Hong Kong and Singapore, though the environment in these places was probably substantially less favorable, given the massive population inflows and sudden structural changes that they were respectively forced to absorb.[2] Again, high growth rates, healthy and hard-working populations, and strong support for the market system, including a willingness to accept large amounts of foreign investment, have been keystones of their development policies. When the subject of China comes up, one might remember that there are four Chinas, three of them capitalist, and that the capitalist Chinas are the more rapidly growing ones.

Success stories about market-based economic development are not limited to China. Mexico has been following this route with great success for three or four decades; so has Puerto Rico, and more recently Brazil has moved to the front rank of the world's growth success stories, following the same institutional pattern. In southern Europe Greece has been a model for this approach to development since shortly after her communists were defeated in a civil war. High-level capitalist performers in other parts of the world include South Korea and Iran. And, of course, there are the older examples such as South Africa and Japan. *No other group of countries in the world, socialist, communist, or what have you, can match the growth performance of the capitalist-market group whose names we have just run through.*

During the last two decades a great deal has been learned about the process of economic modernization. One or two of these lessons is worthy of note, simply to illustrate the general tendency of this experience. Some of the most interesting learning experiences have to do with economic planning. Making plans for the development of national economies became all the rage in the years following World War II. The Soviets were popular models for emulation, and their Five-Year Plans had become symbols of the idea of planned and self-conscious economic change. Also, a large number of political leaders in the newly independent countries thought of themselves as socialists, and all socialists believe that planning has to be better than the market.

These and similar justifications appeared often in the press down through the sixties in underdeveloped countries. But probably they were not the most important reasons why planning came to countries that were not actually conquered by Soviet Russia. In fact, the talk about socialism was mostly lip service; in practice, the politicians were mostly thoroughgoing liberals. They wanted "planning" too, but for different reasons. For example, consider the Keynesian isolationists. These students of Keynes abounded on the left. Their idea was that the Keynesian economic policies could be used to manipulate the economy, but only if the economy itself could be effectively isolated from world markets. Fixed foreign-exchange rates, high tariffs and import quotas, export subsidies, stringent controls over or outright prohibition of private foreign investment: These were the devices that would serve to isolate the economy, to allow the "planner" scope to practice his trade without interference from market signals. To a considerable extent Keynesianism became a sort of power trip; you adjust the economy in such a way as to make you, the planner, most powerful. Make your appeal to independence and nationalism, and the press that supported you would make you into a national hero.

Many leaders in the underdeveloped countries chose this course. The economists they hired to defend their policies gave the policy a technical name: economic development through import substitution. And on the surface, for a while, it worked. The manufacturing sectors of economies under this kind of economic control did develop. But as time went on, a number of problems began to emerge. One of the problems with import substitution is that it concentrated scarce imported capital in industries in which the economy was just not competitive. The result was that the capital imports were not generating foreign exchange to pay off the loans and so debts began to accumulate rapidly, sometimes to the point at which a substantial portion of a country's export earnings were being used merely to pay the interest on the existing debt. Studies began to emerge showing that the economic gains from substitution of domestic manufactures for foreign goods were substantially less than the costs of obtaining the capital initially. For example, behind the high tariff barriers the domestic manufacturer was able to charge a very high price for his goods. One consequence of this was that only the relatively affluent citizen could afford to buy the domestically produced goods. This and the slower real growth meant that income distribution was becoming more skewed rather than less. And so on.[3]

But what, the reader may well be asking, became of those economic planners who were supposed to be controlling the whole process in the interests of the broad mass of the citizenry? The answer is that they never did have much control over the economy, beyond a certain ability to see that funds flowing through the government budget were misspent. Economies are far too complex things to be controlled effectively at a single place. Plans were made, to be sure. Rules and regulations were passed. Controls were slapped on this or that economic activity. The upshot of all this was that some things cost more than they would have without the controls; that some things had to be bought on the black market instead of from the shop window of some big department store; that the poor, with relatively less access to information and less mobility, probably had to pay more for many things and were unable to get others because they were being handed out by bureaucrats sensitive primarily to the interests of the influential. As I write these words the prime minister of Israel has just resigned because his wife maintained a substantial bank account in the United States, something Israeli planners have decreed is illegal. That's the way it goes everywhere under "development planning": There are a lot more rules, many prices are higher, but behavior is not all that much affected. The price is paid in the silent inefficiency caused by the diversion of effort into circumventing the rules.

Over the past ten years these problems have been coming increasingly to light. Conservative development economists, of course, were making the case from the beginning, but their arguments can no longer be ignored.[4] Keynesian economics has never worked well in developed countries; with their greater economic rigidities and generally substantial involvement in world markets, it works even less well in developing countries. Five-year plans, as important as a national airline to the sense of sovereignty of many developing countries, are now recognized as political rather than economic devices, and are rarely implemented. The power of the market to mobilize energies in the service of personal gain is coming, however reluctantly, to be recognized as the driving force behind economic development. This is most promising for the future.

However, it should also be recognized that the fight against economic planning is by its nature a battle that can never be finally ended. Politicans want power, and control of the economy is unquestionably one of the ways in which the politician's power can be increased. His schemes to "foster economic development" may do no more than win him votes from one or two interest groups, but that is basically what he is after. Continuing education in the real consequences of most market intervention can perhaps serve to keep the depredations from getting out of hand.[5]

Probably the single most effective argument used in the service of economic planning is that the market in a developing country is underdeveloped; consequently, the government must intervene to take up the slack or to point the economy in the "right" direction. Most books on economic development that stress the role of planning put principal emphasis on this assertion. It is a very dangerous half truth. There are, in fact, a number of respects in which markets are indeed defective in developing countries. Most of these are a product of deficiencies in the definition or enforcement of property rights or in the costs of establishing them. This can be very discouraging for the energetic and ambitious, for they can see their opportunity slipping away for reasons that have nothing to do with the quality of their product or potential demand. The ill-defined and ill-protected nature of property rights in underdeveloped countries is the major reason why these countries *are* underdeveloped.

Probably the most important factor in restricting property rights in developing countries is disorder. Political turmoil and the consequent risks of confiscation and destruction and weak governments make property rights all too often unenforceable. The existence of large bureaucracies means that rights are ill-defined. And corruption cuts both ways. On the one hand, it raises the costs of transactions; but on the other hand, it means that bureaucratic restrictions on rights can, for a price, be bypassed. Unfortunately, it also means that such rights can, for a price, be infringed. In such an environment peculiar and very inefficient economic arrangements result. In Chile before the junta took over in 1973, the local money, being subject to violent inflation, was saved by no one. People either held foreign currencies or invested in land. Since many landowners were using the land simply as a means of preserving the value of their assets, and the tax system reinforced such behavior, it was often uncultivated and Chile was a substantial importer of food, which diverted foreign exchange that, under a free-market regime, would undoubtedly have gone into investment. In Greece, before the anticommunist government was stabilized in the mid-fifties—and this is also true of many Latin American countries—citizens kept much of their wealth abroad because of fear of confiscation.

Weak development of the market and of property rights is not much of an argument for economic planning. One only has to think for a moment about just what is being put in place of the market. The planner's proposal is to use a bureaucracy. But bureaucracies in underdeveloped countries are also highly "underdeveloped," not in terms of their size, to be sure, but in terms of their ability to define and carry out tasks effectively. For example, the bureaucrat is being asked in effect to substitute his judgment for that of the market in modernizing the country when, obviously, he has no experience of modernization on which to base his judgment. As has been argued in just about every chapter of this book, bureaucracies work rather poorly under the best of circumstances. But a developing country with its low levels of education and experience and its traditions of opposition to trade and markets is very nearly the worst of circumstances. Though in those conventional textbooks of liberal economics it is rarely so argued, it seems clear enough that bureaucracies are an even worse choice than underdeveloped markets as vehicles for economic development. And finally, one might note that bureaucracies are the wrong medicine in a more direct sense. Bureaucracies, as was argued in chapters 6 and 7, have tended to raise the costs of establishing property rights in the United States, and in many other ways to make rights less well defined and enforceable. But if that is the major obstacle to development, applying bureaucracies to the problem can be expected to make things worse, not better!

This is not to argue that there is no role for the state in developing countries. In fact, the state has about the same role there as elsewhere, namely, to establish and protect a system of civil and property rights under the rule of law. This means that, given the relatively ill-defined nature of property rights in such countries, the state may reasonably undertake their improvement. An example or two will illustrate the point. One of the major problems in developing countries, already suggested above, is the relatively poorly developed credit and capital markets. This has led to various types of state intervention. Most successful among these have been actions designed not to substitute for the nonexistent or weak markets but those designed to foster the development of the missing markets. A well-designed development bank, such as has played a major role in Mexico's successful development experience, is a good example. The function of such a bank is to bring together capital and entrepreneurship, both foreign and domestic. The state, in addition, may endow the bank with an initial grant of capital, which the bank can use to buy shares in the new companies. As a project matures and becomes profitable, the market for its shares develops and the state can gradually sell off its holdings, using the proceeds to catalyze other projects. In the early stages there may be some state participation in management decisions, but for success these too must be limited and self-liquidating. After a few decades of intelligent administration of such an agency, it will no longer be true that the capital market is underdeveloped. And no large state bureaucracy has been created, only some new or newly effective markets.

Similar possibilities exist in other areas such as agricultural credit. In Pakistan, for example, a large government bureaucracy was created to administer the allocation of tubewells to farmers. The project bogged down in a variety of ways, none of which did anything to curb the growth of the bureaucracy. Finally, a market solution was tried. The tubewells were simply sold to local dealers. Farmers with good credit who found the tubewell a profitable investment, given the special features of their own farms, bought them, and agricultural production began to increase rapidly. There was no special secret here. The market selection process tended to get the equipment to those best able to use it instead of those who had the most political influence. And the relation of turnover to profit ensured that the wells moved quickly from the dealers' shelves to the users.[6] Some government assistance in setting up credit institutions was necessary, but basically government involvement in the operation was self-liquidating. Such are the models from which a conservative picture of the process of economic development emerges.

What is the future of the underdeveloped countries? In fact, no one can say. There are many difficult problems, and the degree of difficulty varies widely from country to country. There are self-aggrandizing bureaucracies everywhere in the developing world, and so there is still wide resort to ineffective bureaucratic "solutions" to problems. But viewers of the developing world from the United States should remember that there is no such thing as a "widening gap." Counries are moving down the path to development at almost every conceivable rate of change. The more successful of them are growing substantially more rapidly than the already-developed countries. Furthermore, as our list of success stories and their policy orientation shows, the basic ingredient in economic development is self-help. Those who would make us our brothers' keepers are those who in actual effect are hindering the natural processes that can lead to economic development.

CHAPTER 12

The International
Economy

IN RECENT YEARS most major newspapers seem to have made a substantial change in their policies regarding coverage of the international monetary situation. Time was when this was considered to be front-page news, with annual or even more frequent crises getting scare headlines, and with political feature writers giving careful attention to the grave global implications inherent in the latest moves by various governments. Recently, however, there has been a gradual removal of this news to the financial pages and a substantial decline in the amount of punditry that is devoted to such matters.

What is it, some kind of conspiracy? No, it's just another conservative principle at work. One of the most cherished of liberal and radical principles, isolation of the domestic economy from international influences, had been the major factor in generating the hullabaloo all along. In order to preserve this sense of isolation, most countries, including the United States, fixed their rates of exchange between domestic and foreign currencies. This created constant imbalances between the supply and demand for these currencies. Discrepancies had to be paid off by exchanges of gold or by borrowing. Speculators had a field day as they extrapolated an imbalance into a crisis and made the crisis more likely. Eventually, some countries would make a "once-for-all" exchange rate adjustment, and the old crisis would end. But new imbalances would arise almost immediately, thus starting up a new crisis.

For years conservative economists, and in particular Milton Friedman, have been arguing that the fixing of exchange rates has been a major destabilizing influence on international money markets. They have argued for floating exchange rates, in which the supply and demand for the various currencies determined the rates. This has two important advantages over fixed rates. The first is the obvious advantage that the market rate of exchange measures the actual, current relative scarcity of any pair of currencies and so is the most effective rate on which to base economic decisions. The other major advantage is that it gets the hands of government officials out of the monetary mechanism. The politician is bound to have interests different from those who actually trade on international markets, and those different interests have caused much of the trouble. The politician has a short time horizon and he, like others, would like to get something for nothing. This he can do with fixed exchange rates by in effect subsidizing his country's exports while delaying, perhaps through loans or domestic price manipulations and economic controls, the need to pay off the inefficiently high international obligations such a policy entails.[1]

Nowadays individual countries can still get into trouble through spendthrift policies. But the problem does not create a big political crisis. The international markets have probably already discounted most of the difficulty through exchange rate changes before this kind of "crisis" becomes a matter of public discussion. And solution of the problem now depends on the ability of the country involved to convince international lenders that it is a good credit risk. This tends to structure the problem in a way that puts the incentives to change squarely on those who can, in fact, correct it instead of in effect holding the entire international financial community hostage, as was typically done in the days of fixed rates. Britain or Italy can have a crisis now without the international money market having to have one as well. The shift to floating exchange rates did not solve all the problems of international finance, but it has created a sturdier and economically sounder structure for dealing with future problems.

The shift to floating exchange rates was forced on reluctant governments by circumstances. But the fact that conservative economists' predictions were so strongly vindicated in this area, and liberal arguments refuted, has suggested to many people that perhaps some other conservative arguments may be deserving of a hearing. In the area of international economics, there are certainly a number of fundamental differences between conservatives on the one hand and liberals and radicals on the other. Let us take a brief look at a few of them.

If the crises have made themselves scarcer, the past year or two has seen another aspect of international trade begin to grab headlines. This time it is the "problem of the falling dollar." Now, this is not a crisis in the old sense. The specific movements of foreign exchange rates and monetary media in themselves create no immediately serious problem. However, debt does accumulate in the United States and exchange reserves in Germany and Japan and Saudi Arabia, and over a sufficient period of time this could become serious. On a market, of course, such events are supposed to create their own corrective forces: All relative prices adjust until the supply and demand for foreign exchange are again brought into balance. Why is this not happening? The same old answer applies to this different situation: government action. In this case, for example, government price controls on domestically produced oil and natural gas prevent the price of oil from rising and so discouraging demand. And governments continue to intervene to "protect" their currencies and to expand their supplies through deficit spending. Eventually, no doubt, "circumstances" will force the government to recognize once again the ineffectiveness of these de facto interventions in the floating exchange rate system and allow the market to do the job. And conservatives will take what pleasure they can in delivering yet another "I told you so!" to the liberal politicians in power.

Quite possibly the most misleading word in the entire vocabulary of liberal and radical writers is "imperialism." Perhaps the best way to establish this is to remind the reader of a few relatively obvious facts about international economic interactions. Consider first the charge that imperialist countries extract the wealth of the poorer countries and ship it to the developed world at exploitative prices. On its face this is an odd line of argument, since under a market system that is precisely what will *not* happen. If the foods are valuable, the owner of the resource will be able to get a good price for his product by the usual bargaining process. Note that he will probably complain that the price he is getting is too low because, being human, he would prefer to get more for less. But where markets exist, prices tend to be established that reflect relative scarcities. Clearly, the "problem of imperialism" is not associated with the normal functioning of markets.

As a concept imperialism arose to describe the relations between a country and its conquered dependencies. This usage seems reasonable. It has not been uncommon for imperialist—in this sense—countries to impose restrictions on the trade of the colonials to the material benefit of its own citizens. England did that to America in the form of the Navigation Acts. Of course, such colonial dependencies have essentially disappeared from the contemporary free world. However, that is not true of the Soviet bloc. Today the world's great imperial power by this standard is Soviet Russia, which imposes far more extensive and effective restrictions on the international trade of its numerous colonies than capitalism has yet seen. Under capitalism this kind of colonial restrictionism is no longer a matter of significant concern.[2]

A second claim is that "international monopolies" conspire to set prices, thereby abrogating the true scarcity relationships. People who use this line of argument are, of course, referring to the multinational corporations which have grown very rapidly in the last few decades. But there seem to be several fundamental problems with this interpretation. In the first place, there are almost no monopolies among the international corporations; instead, they are in rather keen competition with one another for markets. Most multinational activity has taken place in the already developed countries, especially those of the Common Market, where the opportunities for monopolizing a market are minimal. The profits come from successful operation in a relatively free-market environment. Second, international operation tends to expand the range of competition rather than contract it. American automobile companies were forced to make a number of changes in their products in response to keen competition in the United States from European producers. Or consider East and Southeast Asia, an area where, as already noted, a number of "Third World" countries have been astonishingly successful at carrying out successful economic development, starting from a level of extreme poverty. This is an area where the multinational corporation abounds. Furthermore, American, Japanese, and even British corporations are in keen competition with one another to take advantage of economic opportunities in countries that are generally receptive to foreign investment. Perhaps it is no accident that these two things, rapid development and intense activity by multinationals, seem to go together. One rather obvious reason why this should be so is that modernization requires the transfer of technology from the developed to the underdeveloped countries. The multinationals seem to be relatively well equipped to carry out this task efficiently.

A third aspect of imperialism suggests a rather different issue, namely, the taking advantage in some sense of the weakness of an underdeveloped country. No doubt it is true that if a country is backward and ruled by a corrupt and ignorant leadership, citizens are not likely to fare too well in economic activities in which effective government action is required. But two things might be noticed about this kind of situation. The first is, you can hardly blame that archvillain of radical and left liberal rhetoric, the United States, for such a situation. We are not a colonial power and, in contrast with the situation in Eastern Europe, we are not discussing situations in which the existing government is only maintained in power by foreign troops. These are unfortunate situations, but they are not the product of contemporary "monopoly capitalist imperialism." The second and perhaps more important point is that the burden of this claim is really that the relevant government cannot be relied upon to carry out a policy effectively. This then is an argument against foreign aid, which flows from government to government. And we would be wise to learn from our errors here, where literally billions of dollars of such aid have been wasted by corrupt and inefficient governments.

One final point about "imperialism." An underdeveloped country in which market relations are not highly developed is likely to be one in which property rights are not widely respected. A government that is weak and inefficient is unlikely to be able effectively to define or enforce property rights. This explains much of the relation between, for example, mining companies and developing-country governments during the first half of the twentieth century. Unable to obtain an appropriate supply of services from the underdeveloped local markets, unable to obtain security from the governments, unable to convince the government that infrastructure projects were in the general interest, the companies simply provided these things themselves. The Chilean copper mines are a good case in point. Governments were kept at bay by those devices, including bribery, which constituted the custom of the time and place. This was the only feasible way in which the companies' legally acquired property rights could be enforced.[3]

No doubt there were abuses. Since property rights acquired in such circumstances would be quite fuzzy, the company often had the ability to define or even redefine those rights; no doubt the general tendency in the new definition favored the company's interests. It is rather pointless to attempt to assign blame in such a situation; however, if one must, the most reasonable culprit would seem to be the weak and corrupt government and the domestic population that was prepared to tolerate it. Some measure of self-help is not an unreasonable demand to make on a government and the more influential citizens of a country.

The only alternative to the above process in many countries was to keep the companies out entirely. Many seem to think this was the better alternative. However, the investigations of some development economists suggest that this is clearly false. The companies brought employment, tax revenues, technology, and a growing familiarity with the modern world and its ways. Inevitably, the infrastructure projects did begin to be built. As time went on and the population that had been exposed to these new influences expanded, pressures to reform government and to organize it to assist general domestic modernization grew steadily. It seems clear that, on the whole, these companies did play a substantial role in stimulating the process of economic development. The process can be faulted somewhat, however, if one compares countries that preserved their independence with those that came under colonial rule. In general, the latter had acquired a more substantial infrastructure base for the carrying out of further development than had the former. Obviously, property rights were better protected in the colonies and the governments more concerned with economic development than were the native rulers. Needless to say, this point is typically missed in liberal and socialist accounts of the development process.[4]

Writers in the above two genres have had to do a good deal of scrambling about to new positions in recent years. For example, the classic cases of "imperialist exploitation" inevitably used to be taken from the Middle East, and in all the Middle East no country could match Iran's claimed record of victimization, which even extended to American assistance in bringing down an Iranian government. The role of Iranians in the latter even tends to be ignored, though in fact a great many of them were seriously disturbed over the threat to property rights and, as a consequence, to economic development of the policies of the Mossadegh regime. However, that is not the main point. By no stretch of the imagination can Iran be regarded today as the victim of imperialism. Somehow she has managed to bring the oil companies into a position of collaboration with her sovereign state. She has substantially secured the rights of private investors and used oil revenues to provide the basic structure of a modernized economy. As a result, Iran has had one of the highest rates of economic growth in the world for a period now approaching two decades. Three decades ago Iran was a weak nation and the "victim" of the most powerful of the international companies. Perhaps she should be regarded as the world's healthiest victim!

There is no need to continue this line of argument. Similar stories can be told for most of the countries on the list of success stories in the last chapter. It might be noted that as development proceeds, manufacturing tends to replace mining as the major multinational activity in many developing countries. This means more interdependent involvement of the foreign companies in the economic life of the countries and, consequently, a more rapid spread and deeper penetration of the ideas of modern organization and technology. The message seems clear: Those countries that are prepared to test themselves against the world market are the ones most likely to succeed.

A final word about foreign economic aid is in order. Conservatives are not enthusiastic about the efficiency that can be achieved by government economic activity. Consequently, they tend to be positively frightened at the idea of foreign "aid," which involves economic activity by two governments. The giver's congress appropriates the funds, adjusting the proposals of the executive bureaucracy. The giver's state department negotiates receipt of the funds with the recipient's foreign ministry, which then passes the funds on to the recipient's government bureaucracy to spend. Is it any wonder that students of such programs believe the funds have been largely wasted? At no point in this system of transfers is there a serious confrontation between expected costs and benefits. What it turns out to be is the traditional pork barrel, this time internationalized. An end to foreign economic aid might result in a measurable decline in the number of Mercedes on the streets of some foreign capitals, but probably not much else.

This is not to argue that there is no role for the United States to play vis-à-vis developing countries. The security role is important and will be discussed later. There are some measures of assistance that have been helpful, of which disease control is perhaps the most important. Some assistance in training technicians, both at home and abroad, can probably be done in a way that benefits the recipient nation. Some guarantees of at least a portion of private loans for investment in developing countries may also be justified as a device to stabilize property rights while assisting the essentially private process of industry building. What should be stopped once and for all is the so-called program aid, in which the United States actually requires that the developing country produce an economic plan and we then provide funds to carry it out. This has tended to produce just about everything but the desired effects. For example, in Greece in the early fifties our efforts along this line produced not modern industry but a plethora of high-rise middle-class apartments in downtown Athens.[5]

No doubt those who got newer and cheaper housing were happy, as were the apartment owners; but was it reasonable to extract a billion dollars from the American taxpayer for such a purpose? Much the same can be said for the majority of project-oriented aid, if the mechanism is that same government-to-government transfer. On the average, money is much more wisely spent if the spender is closely associated with both aspects of the venture, its costs and its benefits.

CHAPTER 13

Socialism

SOCIALISM is supposed to be the hope of mankind, the socialist society the place where affluence, justice, equality, brotherly love, and other good things will finally accrue to all. "Socialism" first showed up in Soviet Russia sixty years ago; it has been the way of life for many hundreds of millions of Asians and East Europeans for over a quarter of a century. How well does the reality fit the paper utopia? [1]

The first thing to note about socialism is that nowhere in any socialist society today is the will of the people tested by the government to see whether they like what they've got or not. These regimes were all born in violence and coercion, and they all survive with continued oppression and the rigid suppression of basic civil rights. One is perhaps permitted to suspect that there is some good reason why no people, anytime, anywhere, has freely chosen by majority vote to go socialist.

In terms of economic organization, the most noticeable difference that socialism makes is in the nationalization of industry. However, here as elsewhere, the motivation is much more political than economic. There is, in fact, no economic theory of nationalization that concludes that nationalized industry should perform more efficiently than its privately owned counterpart. Nor is there any evidence that it does perform better. Both theory and practice come to just the opposite conclusion. But nationalization does have very important political consequences It destroys the "bourgeoisie," depriving them of their property rights, their income, and, of course, their political voice. These rights all devolve on the state creating, in place of the competition among capitalists for the consumers' favor, a single large monopoly that controls these and other rights. Judging from their literature, the technical socialist term for this monopoly is "the People," which is undeniably an esoteric use of the word.

In considering the economic aspects of the operation of a socialist economy, probably the best approach is to think of it as if it were a market economy on which has been superimposed a vast maze of constraints. For despite all the oppression and monopolization, socialist states have proven singularly unable effectively to control the giant organization they have created. They have simply bitten off far more than they could chew, organizationally speaking. There are literally millions of goods being produced in a modern economy. Finding out their names and how much of each *can* be produced and what they can be used for and how much of other goods must be used to produce each is a task well beyond the capacities of any currently known group of economic planners. But that is only the start of the task, for the planners are supposed to decide which of the almost infinite combinations of goods that might be produced is the best one from the point of view of the economy's bosses. This requires a theory of production far more sophisticated than any currently existing. It has also been pointed out that even if all the above problems were to be solved at some time in the future, centralized planning might still fail simply because the computation of the "optimal" plan would be infeasible; the numbers of goods to be produced would dissolve as rounding errors gradually dominated the massive calculations.

These facts are well known to economists East and West.[2] It is because of them that the market emerges from behind that vast maze of economic controls. Since the planners cannot do their job correctly, they do a sort of caricature of it, planning the output of groups of commodities. There are several tens of thousands of different products of the steel industry. Planners divided them into perhaps ten groups and fix the amounts of these in the plan. Intermediate-level bureaucrats are responsible for dividing these figures into smaller units, the central planners hope that the proportions among the commodities included in each bundle will remain about the same as they were last year. However, the plan calls for rapid industrial growth, which means substantial changes in the relative outputs of the various goods—much more machinery, not so much more grain. So a basic contradiction is built into the plan from the start. The planners know that it cannot reflect closely the actual outcome.

But the manager has his own set of problems. He is expected to know what is best for the economy even though the national planners themselves do not. He is expected, if there is a shortage of some input he needs, to find hidden reserves in his own production to compensate. He is expected to make adjustments in product specifications to suit the needs of his purchasers. He is expected to produce according to the assigned product mix, but not to pile up stocks of unwanted goods. These are impossible tasks as stated, and the manager soon learns that he is actually expected frequently to violate the plan, because everybody knows that it is a poor reflection of the actual needs of the economy.

But when the manager starts thinking along these lines, he needs some guidelines. In which particular direction should he violate the plan when it becomes clear that plan and reality are far apart? At this point, it turns out that there *are* some prices around to guide his choices. The manager who is unable to obtain needed inputs from the harried planners finds there is a market of sorts in inputs, where he can barter some good he has in surplus for the good he needs. He gets away with this partly because the planners and other government officials cannot look over the shoulder of every bureaucrat to make sure he is doing what he is told. He also gets away with it because higher officials wink at the procedure, knowing that it is essential to the operation of the system, given the poor quality of the planning.

However, the process does not stop there. So far we have not mentioned the worker-consumer. He—she too, for in socialism everyone gets to work whether they want to or not—gets paid wages like his capitalist counterpart and goes to stores to spend his money in the same way. But as the socialist worker approaches the store, one of the big differences between socialism and capitalism emerges. There are very few goods in the socialist store, and there are long lines waiting to get many of those. A Czech study estimated that an average urban family spent more than a dozen hours a week standing in line. However, some of the shelves will be full of goods; these are overproduced items that nobody wants, and stocks of them may grow in stores and warehouses for months before the bureaucratic process grinds out the order to stop. Faced with this environment, consumers have several possible courses of action. They can first try to set up a private information network that will give them early warning that some desired commodity is about to appear somewhere so they can get in near the front of the line. They can use influence to get moved up on the waiting lists for such things as cars and apartments. They can engage in illegal sales and trades among themselves. And they can keep an eye out for a foreign traveler, or for the opportunity to travel. Travelers from abroad are beset with offers for everything they bring with them, including literally the shirts off their backs; travelers to the "outside" come back laden like Santa Claus with the domestically unobtainable goods they have found in abundance on capitalist shelves.

But the process of market emergence does not stop here. Producer and consumer can be brought into interaction. A "second market" emerges in which goods produced illegally are among the many items for sale. Whole factories have been discovered that produce goods with inputs siphoned off illegally from a socialist factory, which are then sold for private profit on the second market. According to recent émigrés, the officials who are supposed to prevent such things from happening are among the more enthusiastic participants in the second market; no wonder, since they are more likely to have more money to spend. It is in almost everyone's interest to wink at the second market.[3] But even the government can find ways to use this emergent market. One way is to set up special stores in which only hard currency can be spent, thus getting back under government control some of the fruits of illegal trade. Visas to travel have been sold in China, as no doubt have many other kinds of government permissions.

But this second market is a very inefficient one. In particular, it should be noted that property rights are not well defined or enforced since so much of the activity is clandestine. The constraints show up in empty shelves where goods are supposed to be available, and in the ever-present queues. They also show up in poor-quality goods. Perhaps best known of the empty-shelves stories is the annual complaint heard in the Soviet Union that at the peak of the harvest season up to half of the tractors are unusable because there are no spare parts.

A few years ago, during the brief months of the "Prague spring," a Czech economist reported that Czechoslovakia produced over 200 commodity groups for export but none of them was competitive with world- (i.e., capitalist-) market quality standards.[4] All estimates of output per capita in socialist countries should be reduced by some unknown but substantial amount to take account of this tremendous waste and poor quality, for it does clearly make the output far less useful to the consumers. The basic cause of all this inefficiency is, of course, the cumbersome and ineffective system of controls. They serve to prevent arbitrage, that is, bargaining over price and quantity and quality, by the various potential producers and users of a good. The price system works fitfully and no one is very secure in his property rights. A sudden efflorescence of production in one part of the system, a sudden deterioration of quality somewhere else, a sudden crack-down by the authorities in a third, a sudden demand for a cut by some official in a fourth: By such events are property rights and efficiency whittled away and consumer wants ignored in this deformed market economy we call socialism.

If this system is so inefficient, why do socialist regimes stick with it? After all, they do want the goods for military purposes and to keep their subject peoples from becoming restive if for no others. Furthermore, in private discussions with economists from these countries, one often hears them conclude that substituting markets for bureaucracies is their personal prescription for solving these major ills. There even were some halting movements in that direction in most socialist countries during the sixties. But they were swiftly aborted and the bureaucracies retained. The reasons once again seem to be political rather than economic. A market economy is inevitably a relatively open one, and that poses a political threat to the socialist regime it is simply not willing to accept. This fear is not a figment of the leaders' imaginations. There have, after all, been several revolutions staged against socialist governments. These have been grassroots affairs, such as the Berlin riots in the early fifties, or the Polish October, or the already mentioned Prague spring of Dubcek, or the strike of the Polish dockworkers, or the recent wave of strikes and riots in China. For the regime to survive, the mixture of brutal suppression and occasional concessions must be maintained. A market would require relations with foreign countries. Mobility and communication would expand and include ever-widening sectors of the population. As socialist workers compared their lot with that of Western workers, they would come to realize the heavy material price they have had to pay for socialism. Nowhere is this contrast more striking than the comparison between Austria and Czechoslovakia. In the years just following World War II, it was clear that the standard of living in Czechoslovakia was far above that in Austria. Then in 1948 the communists staged a coup and brought the blessings of socialism to Czechosolvakia. Twenty years later it was clear that the situation with respect to living standards had been almost precisely reversed. In 1968 the Czechs tried to move back toward a more open market society. The Russians, fearing that if the Czechs succeeded all the rest of the socialists would not be far behind, intervened with their troops and put the old regime back in. Without those Russian troops, East Europe would undoubtedly be capitalist today.

One of the more amusing aspects of socialism is the fickleness of Western radical fashions with respect to the question as to which of the socialist countries is the true model for all the rest of us to follow. However, closer examination reveals that there is a rule of thumb that offers quite good predictions as to which country will be this year's Givenchy of socialism: The less information the rulers of a socialist country allow to leak out to the West, the more likely the country is to win the competition. During the days of Stalinist slaughter of the innocents, the Soviet Union was Western socialism's official darling. In Castro's early years, little was known about what was actually happening in Cuba, partly because the *lider* had not yet revealed his hand, and all kudos went to Havana. Considerable information about China was allowed out by Mao and company in the fifties. But beginning in 1959, a lid was clamped on almost all publication of useful and revealing information and, sure enough, within a few years Western socialists had leaped on the Maoist bandwagon. By the seventies, however, there was enough known about almost every socialist regime to turn even socialists off—though we must except the tiny but apparently growing band who follow our rule of thumb and believe the true leader of contemporary international socialism is the prime minister of Albania! At the moment no red god rules the sky, though perhaps some former Portuguese African colony will generate another titan, provided he can keep the newsmen at bay.

Is there any fire behind all this smoke in the form of real differences among socialist countries? It would seem not. The lack of corruption in China on the scale that is so obvious in the Soviet Union and Eastern Europe may be entirely a figment of our relative inability to observe China. Or it may be partly due to the fact that China is a much poorer country, so that there are fewer goods to purloin. Or it may be that Chinese are simply a harder-working people—they are exemplary workers wherever they are found in Asia or America. But it should be remembered that they are a strongly family-centered people and that they have demonstrated an extraordinary ability to use the capitalist system for their benefit. It would be surprising indeed if these striking features of Chinese behavior outside the area of communist control find no reflection in their behavior inside.

Perhaps the only real socialist maverick is Yugoslavia, which never collectivized agriculture and which still uses markets and trading among socialist firms. How much real "worker management" there is in that country is a matter of speculation. What one can say is that where the market is allowed to work in Yugoslavia, one sees higher efficiency and better quality goods. Where it is not allowed to work, and especially in the area of investment and finance, problems emerge. Yugoslavia is a sort of halfway house that lends further evidence in support of conservative views about the relation between markets and property rights and genuine prosperity.

CHAPTER 14

International Order

IT WOULD BE nice if the incentives of the market system were always such that the use of coercion never paid off. Unfortunately, that is not the case. Contract law and criminal law are needed to deter fraud and force in the transfer of property rights. And, clearly, the method used by the law is coercion. Of course, the aim of the law is to avoid the actual use of coercion by deterring such acts. It is conceivable, if somewhat unlikely, that a rule of law could develop that would in fact eliminate the actual use of force, in which the deterrence was always successful. But that would not imply the elimination of coercion from society; the threat of force against violations of the law would still be at the basis of deterrence.

Essentially, the same remarks apply on the international scene. There are times when it is useful for those influencing a government's policies to take coercive action. It would be nice if an international system could be devised in which it was never in a nation's interest to seize the property of others forcibly but, realistically, no one knows how to do that. An international free-market system would help a great deal, but it would not eliminate the use of force. Indeed, international as well as domestic markets have a need for some sort of deterrent force in order to function properly. And one cannot ignore the possibility, even the probability, that the entity that will need to be deterred is a nation state.

The international use of force is an area where perhaps more wishful thinking occurs than anywhere else in the study of policy. But conservative principles can serve as an effective means to break through to the basic principles that must guide policy in this area.[1] First, once again, the principle, Keep it simple! One of the greatest dangers in international affairs, when threats of force are being bandied about, is miscalculation based on misinformation or faulty expectations. Simple policies are easier to understand, easier to appraise, easier to get one's opponent to understand, and about all that a government "crisis-management team" can effectively handle.

The first element of wishful thinking and misunderstanding that we will take up has to do with the problem of order in developing countries. It can take the form of a Tale of Two Juntas, namely, those of Greece and Chile. Both these juntas came to power under conditions of rapidly deteriorating public order. Both restored public order promptly. Both took strong measures to stabilize the also deteriorating economic situation, the Greek junta with striking and quick success, the Chilean junta with less success as of the present writing, though the economic situation appears far more promising now than just before it assumed power. Both juntas have been almost universally denounced, nowhere more so than in the United States. They are particularly blamed for systematically violating human rights and for acts of violence. What lessons do these experiences have to teach us?

The first lesson has to do with the selective bias of the liberal press in the United States. How do the acts of violence of these juntas compare with those of other regimes? As far as the Greek junta is concerned, one would have to look around quite carefully to find a society that resorted less to prison and intervention in citizen rights than did this one. Even the claims of its most bitter enemies were rather modest: a few thousand Greeks jailed briefly, a few hundred for a period of years. There is no communist country with a record of jailings as light as this, but, of course, the same liberals who were busy denouncing the Greek junta were simultaneously demanding that the United States establish friendlier relations with several of these far more oppressive regimes.

The Chilean issue is somewhat different. There the junta was intervening in a genuinely revolutionary situation. The rapid deterioration of the economy and the steady spread of extralegal methods, especially including trade union controls over and siphoning of funds from industry that was still, at law, legally owned by private citizens, was moving Chile rapidly toward a point of no return. The junta turned things around and moved the country back toward the situation as it had existed some years earlier. But it faced an organized socialist and communist political movement that was sworn to revolution and to the seizure of all private capital. Unions and the far left had established paramilitary organizations, designed to control the poor and working-class neighborhoods and to resist any attempts to abort the revolution. Illegal acts were a daily occurrence. The violence that accompanied the seizure of power and the restoration of property rights to private citizens must be judged against the standards of other revolutionary situations. Once again we find liberals willing to condone thousands, even millions of deaths in places such as Russia and China and Cuba, while denouncing the deaths that occurred in Chile. Little or no notice is given of the fact of success in Chile: Instead of lingering waves of violence, terror, and assassination, Chile is quiet, in striking contrast with its neighbor, Argentina, or with the violence that has riven so many countries that have been forced under the socialist yoke. Just because the initial measures taken were strong, the amount of violence actually used was relatively modest, given the conditions, and the restoration of order swift. All this happened several years ago and was given much play in the press; however, it would not surprise me if many readers are hearing this argument for the first time.

There is one thing that must be said in favor of the general liberal attitude of vociferous condemnation of authoritarian rightist regimes in developing countries and toleration or even affection for leftist authoritarian regimes. There is an implication about the future in this attitude. Liberals, after all, *do* support the idea of democracy, and their denunciation of right-wing regimes is based on their feeling that it would be better to have democracy and that perhaps they can push these rightist regimes in the direction of more democratic processes. Their tolerance of leftist tyranny is partly based on a tacit recognition that there is no hope of democracy growing out of the rigid and all-embracing oppression of leftist dictators. The conservative shares this feeling that democracy is more likely to grow out of rightist than of leftist regimes; but he also feels that the liberals' attitude is unrealistic and counterproductive.

This point too is illustrated by the two juntas. In both countries there were leaders of the moderate left who were especially disruptive in their political activities. The Papandreous in Greece were liberal or "democratic socialist" in their orientation, while Allende in Chile represented socialists and "moderate" communists. However, by both refusing to accept the existing order and being unable or unwilling to impose a different order, their behavior served to promote disorder. After the fact it seems clear that they, rather than the far left, represented the forces that generated broad public acceptance of military rule.

This is the basic problem of moderates and democrats in most developing countries: They can't fish and they won't cut bait. For the most part, these countries have no tradition of orderly transfer of political power. Property rights and civil rights both are relatively underdeveloped. But economic development can only occur if some orderly processes can be instituted. Since modernization relies on the importation of foreign technology, an orderly relationship with world markets and the more developed world is essential. And rapid change, once it begins, may tend to make stability all the harder to achieve. In this context an authoritarian regime is often the only one that is capable of preserving order. Given the relative levels of oppression involved, the right-wing regime is generally preferable. Property rights are preserved and rightist-ruled societies tend to be more open than their leftist counterparts. Thus the prospects for a more democratic future tend to be greater.

The contrast between regimes such as Brazil and Chile and Greece and Mexico and South Korea on the one hand, and Poland or Bulgaria or Czechoslovakia or North Korea on the other is very striking. In each of the communist countries either the Russians or their local creatures have imposed a regime that more or less replicates the institutions of the Soviet Union, from national plans to secret police. Private property rights, the right to dissent, personal security: All these things disappear. Peasants are herded onto collective farms and milked of their economic surplus to support the regime and its grand designs, which always include an extremely powerful military and police system. Contact with the outside world is reduced to a bare minimum so that the local population has as little opportunity as possible to compare its lot with that of others. Punishment of dissidence is swift and severe, and the regime attempts to control even the thoughts of the populace, especially through strict indoctrination from early childhood.

There are some notable contrasts between this and the authoritarian regime of the right. Already mentioned have been property rights and acceptance of foreign investment. In general, these regimes are much more open to foreign influences and their populations have much greater opportunity to travel. The family is strongly supported as a primary social institution; as a consequence, state indoctrination is less intensive. Indeed, the typical rightist regime does not care too much what its citizens believe just so long as they do not organize against the government. And the range of political viewpoints in the literature permitted to be distributed within the country is far wider than in communist states.[2]

What should United States policy toward authoritarian regimes be? The above arguments suggest that both self-interest and humanitarian concern for the future of these peoples dictate a general policy of support for authoritarian regimes of the right but not of the left. And we have not yet mentioned another and often decisive factor. The United States seeks friends among the nations of the world, who will not only welcome economic relations with us but will serve also as friends or allies when it comes to confrontation with our enemies. And here, of course, the situation requires no argument at all. We have a common interest with most authoritarian regimes of the right in preventing the spread of communism and the expansion of the power and the influence of our enemies. In this case the most important and relevant dimensions all point in the same direction. Were due respect given to conservative principles, there would be relatively few dilemmas in constructing a proper foreign policy with respect to developing countries.

Surely enough has been said by now to lay to rest notions that developments in the world are influenced by something called "American imperialism." Authoritarian regimes come to power in developing countries for reasons associated either with internal developments or with subversion from without by communists. Under liberal aegis, American governments have by and large opposed right-wing authoritarian regimes, at least until they come to power and not infrequently thereafter. Among the most successful of developing countries (remember the list of chapter 11) are those that have had the closest relations with the United States and with American and other foreign private investment. In Greece, Mexico, and elsewhere, one can see not only economic development but a movement toward more open and ultimately democratic political orders as the process of development in close interconnection with world markets proceeds. Nowhere does one see the process of economic development moving developing countries toward greater dependence on the United States; again, the truth is just the opposite of the common view instilled by liberal pundits and media.

To this point we have been considering American relations with countries that do not have the military capacity seriously to threaten the United States.[3] We must now turn to the question of the relation of the United States to its enemies and the relation, in turn, to the problem of international order. Identifying one's enemies is a simple matter. One has only to ask: What countries have the military capability to hurt seriously the United States? The answer, good for the present and also for some years into the future is: Soviet Russia has that capacity, and China is trying hard to acquire it. And that is the end of the list, suggesting where primary attention must be devoted in thinking about national defense. What governments that have the capacity to hurt you seriously say about their intentions is always interesting, but it is never so decisive as the existence of that capacity. For intentions can be concealed, especially in a closed society, or they can change, and on much shorter notice than can the military capacity successfully to defend oneself.

The second simple question is: What should the United States do about it? Again the basic answer is as simple as the question: Deter. Create a military establishment that has the capacity to ensure that an enemy attempt to use force has no hope of producing any net advantage to that enemy. Creation of such a force, of course, implies a credible commitment to using it if necessary.

The third question is a little less simple: What do we do about international violations of the property rights of Americans? The answer can get a bit complicated, but roughly it goes: Establish a system of civil penalties to deal with such violations, using and developing international agencies of adjudication where possible, but developing a national system where necessary. An implication of this formula is that the U.S. marines are not available to enforce American property rights abroad, but that an adversary system of resolving such conflicts is available to the parties involved. Since governments that have just, say, nationalized U.S. property are not likely to be willing to submit themselves to an American court over the issue, acts of government policy are probably unavoidable. But the sanctions should be kept civil in nature so long as the violation is of rights of property rather than person.

This covers the essential points involving the use of force in international relations. Of course, in practice things are complex and uncertain. The function of simple rules such as these is to make sure that policy development and implementation is carried out with constant awareness of the *principal* goals. And these goals reflect the essentially peaceful thrust of the market system. A functioning and stable market system is one in which all the principal actors have a stake in the continuation of the status quo, with adjustments proceeding at a pace and in a way that does not threaten the stability of the system. The greater the willingness of the other states to avoid the use of force, the better the market will function. And the rewards of a better functioning market to all parties will serve to stimulate the push in the direction of peaceful resolution of disputes. The history of Soviet-American relations over the last quarter of a century can be used to illustrate the validity of the three simple answers as well as this last point.

One final question is perhaps worthy of comment, namely, the persistence throughout this chapter in putting the United States at the center of consideration, the use of the word "we" to refer only to Americans. Why not adopt an internationalist perspective? After all, markets are not at all sensitive to the nationalities of the participants.

The answer to this question is, first, that the perspective *is* internationalist, in the sense that the proposals, while serving the interests of the United States, are certainly not inconsistent with the goals of the rest of the world. An international market system operating within a world order in which the use of force is successfully deterred; who— aside from doctrinaire socialists—could reasonably object to that?

But second, the United States is an entity that is of great importance to all Americans. It serves, more than any other agency outside the market itself, to define the civil and property rights of Americans. It would be nice to have such rights defined on a worldwide basis, but nobody knows how to do that. History and technology seem to decree that this at present is the job of the nation-state. We are fortunate in having one that is large enough to permit efficient markets to function and diverse enough to give us a good taste of the benefits of a dynamic and creative society that such diversity produces, benefits far in excess of their cost in misunderstanding and conflict. There is simply no way to dispense with it at present. Without the United States, we would be missing some of the basic institutions of a thoroughgoing market economy, quite aside from the threat from external predators. The commitment to America is not one of jingoism, but one of common interest, with factors of common heritage playing a strong but supporting role.

CHAPTER 15

The Future

THOUGH it is fading in the seventies, there still remains a strong residue from the days when conservatives were thought to be people whose heads were turned fixedly toward the past. Too many conservatives' positions have been vindicated by events in the last decade or two for that claim to hold much water these days. But one still frequently encounters the view that history is against conservatism, that "the imperatives of technology and organization," as Galbraith calls it, will push us inevitably in the liberal/radical direction. In this chapter we look at a few futurology-type issues to see just how wrong those views seem to be on present evidence.

First, the issue of national defense. As our experience with the Russians increases, this issue has become quite a bit less controversial. Everyone these days is for a strong national defense, and just about everyone realizes that the Russians are our major enemy and that they pose a serious threat. What a contrast with the situation only a decade or so ago, when liberals were proclaiming the end of the cold war! But there is still a problem with pessimists who argue that there is really no hope of avoiding nuclear war, that such a war will destroy us, and who would then rather spend their energies dealing with other things than confronting this awful "fact". This can be a very dangerous position, since it probably will produce neglect of the military, which in turn would sharply increase the by no means sure chance of nuclear war.

The issue essentially hinges around the direction of technical change and its nuclear implications. From the point of view of defense policy, there are basically only three possibilities. One is that the defense wins, that is, that new technology such as laser beams will make it possible to destroy an enemy launch before the missiles have left home territory. The appropriate policy is clear enough: Any possibilities in this direction should be explored and developed posthaste, even if they should prove to be very costly. The second possibility is that we continue in the present situation as new technology emerges. That is, the offense cannot be prevented from successfully detonating nuclear weapons on American territory, but we can maintain an ability to launch a second strike, after absorbing the attack, sufficiently strong that it would make the initial attack pointless from the point of view of the enemy. To maintain this position requires that we continually monitor and develop new possibilities in weaponry. There is no price tag on this effort, but it must suffice to be a genuine deterrent to an enemy leadership that has shown its willingness to commit mass murder upon its own population. The third and most troubling possibility is that offense wins; that is, that technology begins to emerge that suggests an enemy willing to make a first strike can hit its opponent sufficiently hard that an effective second strike will be impossible. But surely the basic strategy even here is clear. If such capacity becomes feasible we can expect the Russians to try to achieve it. Our only effective counter is to try to develop it ourselves, while continuing efforts to improve second-strike efficiency. If we have kept our technological guard up, we should be able to develop such a weapons system quicker and better than the Russians, who still have quite a creaky modern technological capability. At that point negotiations might be in order; but only with secure inspection could such negotiations be allowed to produce even a slackening in our efforts to produce that first-strike-victory capability.

Those are the alternatives the nuclear age and communism have thrust upon us. Though the stakes are much larger, the basic issues are not much different from those faced by some ancient city-state, Athens perhaps, or even Troy or early Rome, when confronting the threat of an enemy who would like to obliterate them. We must face the issue squarely. What we need not do is face it from a position of weakness. Our enemy has not demonstrated a taste for war regardless of outcome. Rather, he acquires force in order to subjugate. A strong defense is the best and only incentive we can give him to avoid the use of force against us.

Information is another area where many feel the trend is inevitably toward centralization and the abridgment of freedoms. But, in fact, the recent trends suggest that Big Brother theory is wrong here. For example, the history of the computer has moved in a direction precisely opposite to these expectations. Its principal uses so far have been to support the decentralization of large organizations into a looser collection of task-oriented groups. The big computer in Washington or New York that was to provide the needed information to run the economy or the government has not yet made its appearance and perhaps never will. At the moment, even firms that have purchased large computers to centralize their operations are moving away from this sort of information system to minicomputers allotted individually to, for example, branch banks. These computers, of course, can "communicate" with one another, but the ability to store and process information in ways appropriate to the local situation is becoming more economical rather than less as a result of the trend toward computer decentralization.

More generally, the information revolution is making information cheaper to acquire, store, and use by several orders of magnitude, as compared with only a few decades ago. That trend will continue for a while in this area, which does not make heavy demands on energy as an input. But information is what markets thrive on. Making it cheaper makes them work better. And as noted in chapter 5, this latter tendency is much weaker for government, so once again the current trend of technology seems to favor the conservative idea of using government less and markets more to deal with our problems of resource allocation.

The relation between economy and government is, of course, a major place where conservatives are thought to have their heads in the sand. And if one simply looks at changes in the size of government over the last half century, one might be inclined to agree. If the share of government spending out of GNP continues at its past rate of increase, by 2019 the government will be purchasing an amount equal to the entire 1977 output of the economy. But there are growing signs that this will not happen. As the property-rights arguments for structuring and limiting government-economy relations find a wider audience, there is reason to expect a reversal of trend. That trend toward increased understanding of the problem is on a strong upturn in academic and business circles and among the general population, where it has perhaps always been strongest. The tax revolt of 1978 is only the most recent manifestation of this tendency.

There is one place, however, where the conservative may despair over the prospects of his educational campaign, and that is the Congress. A simple principle, actually a truism, is, Scarce things *will* be costly. Congress seems truly incapable of mastering this elementary point. It seems to feel that if, for example, oil becomes scarce, it can pass a law calling for rationing, and then people will not have to pay the higher price. Congressmen simply refuse to consider the costs of operating the rationing system, the taxes needed to carry the subsidies of favored consumers, or the even higher prices paid on the inevitable black market as being costs related to their law, costs that do in fact accrue in varying degrees to all citizens as a result of the use of oil.

But, of course, this is an exaggeration. Most of the congressmen who support such schemes for energy, medical care, welfare, and all the rest know very well what they are doing. They are engaged in a quite deliberate process of using issues essentially concerned with efficiency as means for the redistribution of income. They are aware that the voters will not buy direct confiscations of income and are strongly opposed to higher taxes. So congressmen turn to issues such as energy and are willing to pay a considerable price in efficiency in order to get their redistributive aims achieved through the back door. And so the problem here is not to convince the congressmen of conservative principles but to explain to the voters just what their congressmen are doing. That seems quite a manageable task.

"Environmentalism" has become the fashionable code word these days for a whole series of efforts designed to increase the size of government at the expense of the private sector. Wherever the environmentalist looks he sees troubles. People litter, factories pollute. Those are the basics, from which a detailed appraisal of the deficiencies of self-interested behavior will be supplied for any desired sub-group on demand. And, of course, the only possible correction is government prohibition of the activity, unless it is nationalization of the activity. The attractive thing about the environmentalist position is that the lists provided generally do constitute lists of things that are wrong. It can be great fun pointing out other people's defects, and, since nobody is perfect, a small amount of research will produce a rich harvest of deficiencies. Once the idea became fashionable one could be sure that the long lists would be forthcoming.

Of course, the problem with environmentalism is equally obvious. When it comes to proposing solutions for the problems, by and large environmentalists literally don't know what they are talking about. The reason for this is that they are generally referring to very complex phenomena that have many causes and many and scattered effects, none of which have been very comprehensively studied. In considering the consequences of doing one thing or another, they are dealing with something about which no one is qualified to speak.

The history of the most fashionable environmental issue, that pertaining to the automobile, is certainly a case in point, and one that has proved a bit humbling to the more honest among the environmentalists. In the first place, the trend toward smaller cars began in the United States well before the environmentalists had captured the media. The reason was simple enough: The costs of operating a large, luxurious automobile had been rising rapidly. The number of people who had other things they preferred to do with the few hundred dollars a year savings from driving a Volkswagen "bug" began to increase fairly rapidly in the late fifties. This trend has continued with only brief interruptions ever since, and does not seem to be much affected by environmentalism. Furthermore, the demands for rigid controls of emissions, which were nonnegotiable for the environmentalists in the sixties, suddenly seemed rather silly when the oil price rise showed them—and the rest of us—a very different set of relative costs, while controls served to reduce gas mileage. Their response was to demand mandated technologies that would both reduce emissions and increase gas mileage. But more or less normal technological progress in the worldwide and highly competitive automobile industry began in the seventies to yield its fruits, including cars such as the Honda, that could meet high emission standards and get excellent gas mileage without adding a lot of emission-control gadgetry to the cars. The market seems to have been able to adapt in its usual way to market signals, and most of the environmentalist agitation seems to have been either misdirected or unnecessary or both.[1]

This in itself is enough to make one sceptical of environmental proposals, but there is another problem at least as serious, namely, the institutional side of the remedies they propose. The tacit assumption is almost always that the market cannot do the job and that government can. The conservative's explicit and carefully argued thesis is that most of the time the very opposite is true. If there is, in fact, a significant environmental failure, the first place to look is to government itself, to see whether the problem is not largely a consequence of government rigging or restricting of markets. If that is not the case, the next step is to see whether the problem does not stem from inadequately defined or enforced property rights. If this is the case, government action may be feasible to correct it, but the correction will be such as to make the existing markets function better, not to substitute a government bureaucracy for the market. Rare indeed will be the environmental problem that will survive the tests of severity, understanding, market rigging, and property-rights prescription and thus become a legitimate object of direct government intervention. In all likelihood application of these tests to all known environmental problems would result in a substantial reduction in the level of government economic activity.

Yet another big fashion these days is doomsday. Leading this pack is the pseudoscience of the Club of Rome projections of future levels of economic activity, which predict something approaching total economic disaster in about the second decade of the twenty-first century if we, the world, continue on our present course. The best way to think about this problem is to recall a prediction made by a Harvard historian of science a decade or so ago. He pointed out that if the number of scientists continued to grow at its then-current rate, then at about the time of the Club of Rome catastrophe there would be seven scientists per capita in the world! The Club of Rome stuff is of a piece with this prediction with only one exception—the Harvard man was joking. Already, as the world adjusts to higher oil prices, we see the way in which the market system will provide an effective counter to the threat of "disaster" brought on by depletion of a resource. The price of that resource rises and people start seriously looking around for substitutes. Much the same happens or should happen when some problem such as pollution associated with some particular economic activity becomes unpleasant. Those harmed are having their property rights damaged, and should be able to obtain redress; most of the time the redress should consist of higher costs to the producer in order to bring his costs of doing business in line with the true social costs of doing business. Then the market system will create the incentives to improve the situation, by some combination of product substitution, industrial and human migration, and absorption of some level of unpleasantness that is more than compensated by the accompanying benefits. If it weren't for the market's periodic redirections, we would already have passed through a number of Club of Rome-type catastrophes. With its assistance we will be able to avoid this one too.

The main point of this section is a very simple one: Underlying trends in the twentieth century are not at all unfavorable to the flowering of the thoroughgoing market economy. As was noted in chapter 3, the principal technical changes, relating as they do to lowering the cost of communicating and transferring goods and men, have been very favorable toward improving substantially the quality of the market economy over its nineteenth-century counterparts. The United States is supposed to be the central place in the world for the defense of the capitalist system. But it may well be true that a substantial majority of our better-educated citizenry has never been exposed to the major arguments in favor of the system of liberty and its central social manifestation, the thoroughgoing market economy. Once this defect is corrected, by strictly voluntary actions that infringe no citizen's freedom, the potential those underlying forces have created will finally become realizable.

PART II

Commentary

CHAPTER 16

Introduction

THE BASIC PRINCIPLES of conservatism have played an important role in the history of the past millennium and more. Nevertheless, like other orientations toward society and social change, conservatism has also had its ups and downs. For example, nineteenth-century Britain and the United States were far more consonant with the principle of freedom in their economic arrangements than either nation has been thus far in the twentieth century. Much the same thing can be said, with respect to those countries and to many others, for the status of the family.[1]

Within the twentieth century there have also been marked fluctuations in the public and intellectual esteem with which conservative ideas have been held. The twenties were a peak period for the public fortunes of conservatism and the depression thirties and wartime forties a sort of nadir. The widespread public disesteem, and perhaps more fundamental difficulties as well, had their effect on intellectual conservatism, which also reached a low ebb during this period and into the fifties in the United States. This is not to say that conservative voices were silent but rather that they were dispersed and at odds with one another. Conservatism was not One but Many.[2]

In fact, it was Three, three strands of thought whose proponents came from different places, intellectually speaking, and could at first find little or no common ground. The first of these was the libertarian view. Though a main-line inheritor of the tradition of nineteenth-century laissez-faire, this view had suffered a number of apparently decisive defeats in the several decades preceding the fifties. The inability of the major countries to get back onto a normally functioning gold standard as the medium of international exchange during the interwar period had created a strong backlash in favor of "managed" currencies and foreign exchange rates. A number of scandals relating to the behavior of business leaders during the thirties had somewhat tarnished the public image of conservatism, despite the irrelevance of occasional individual malfeasance to the fundamental issues. Probably this tarnished image was more a consequence of the depression itself, which liberal intellectuals had convinced themselves was a product of the failure of the market system. And finally, there was the Keynesian "revolution," which seemed to many to have established the case for big government, big deficits, and national planning. In the increasing turmoil of depression and war, it was becoming increasingly difficult to hear the conservative voices; and, as often happens in such circumstances, these isolated voices, in their attempts to emphasize principle, tended to move toward extreme positions, leaving out the qualifications that actually strengthen the case for those willing to take the time to think about what they have heard.

A second strand consisted of the traditionalist conservatives. Their emphasis was on the role of civilization as the basis for a decent human society. The unfolding two-thousand-year tradition of Judeo-Christian civilization has been the fundamental shaper of European and American—and a number of other—ideas and institutions. In the relativistic and polyglot and materialistic environment that was growing by leaps and bounds, there seemed to be little hope for the continuation of this influence. Churches were not only disestablished but emptying. Universities were steadily sloughing off their role as the conservator and transmittor of the culture to become smorgasbords of vocational training and self-indulgence. Political institutions were in the hands of demagogues and opportunists. For the traditionalists, the basic problem was to mobilize those individuals still knowledgeable of and committed to civilized values for the effort to move conservation in this most fundamental sense to its former central place. At best this was a task for the long run, and it did not leave much time to worry about the details of economic arrangements.

The third strand was anticommunism. A number of writers, many of them formerly active on the left, had come to recognize the severity of the threat of Soviet Russia to Western civilization in general and the United States in particular. It was not just that the Soviets had through terror and organization developed a massive and predatory instrument for imperialist expansion, nor even that this was accompanied by a far more effective fifth column of subversives within the Western democracies than anything that had preceded it. There was also a fundamental lack of recognition of the nature and extent of this threat by the politically dominant liberals. This was the era in which Maoists were spoken of as mere "agrarian reformers," and in which many liberals refused to believe the truth of the great purges in Stalin's Russia, or of the massacres of Poles and others carried out by the various terrorist militias of the Soviets. The sense of desperation felt by those who did perceive the danger once again left little time or energy to devote to the issues raised by conservatives of the other strands.

These are the three strands that form the intellectual base on which the contemporary American conservative movement rests. They have been brought together both by events and by "fusionist" arguments, but also simply by a growing recognition by members of each group of the extensive common ground they share.[3] One major force in the coming together has been the Mont Pélerin Society. Founded in 1947 at a meeting in Switzerland and holding more or less annual meetings since that time, it has been a sort of rallying point for proponents of the free society. Its members have a variety of views, as befits a group emphasizing the value of individualism, but its efforts have served to bring these arguments into the mainstream of discussion and to develop that recognition of common interests and beliefs among conservatives that was essential to further progress. Friedrich Hayek and Milton Friedman, perhaps the two leading conservative economists of recent times, have been active in the society from the start.[4]

The ideas of two economists in particular were very important in this early shaping of the contemporary conservative economic world view. Ludwig von Mises, Hayek's teacher, put the idea of the market economy as man's most effective instrument for economizing, and socialism as an idea that in principle was fatally flawed, at the center of his world view. In several massive volumes Mises developed these two strands into a powerful and integrated theory that emphasizes the rationalism of the one and the irrationalism of the other. The thickness of his books may have kept Mises from reaching a wide audience, but the basic message shows the fundamental link between the first and third of the above conservative strands, between libertarianism and anticommunism.

An author whose influence was probably even greater, though not so often mentioned in this context, is Joseph Schumpeter. In a writing career that spans the first half of the twentieth century, Schumpeter articulated a unique and brilliantly defended theory of the basic political and economic forces at work in our era. His approach was dynamic and emphasized the creativity of the market, its ability to release energies both by releasing men from the trammels of traditional political restraints and by the opportunities for reward that inhere in it. A vital factor for Schumpeter is the role of the family. He sees the founding of a "dynasty" as a central human motivation and one that, again, the market supports. He developed a theory of democratic government that showed clearly the degeneration that was bound to set in if government was required to make too many decisions. We will return to some aspects of his very rich theory in chapter 18; for the moment it is enough to note that, though not an organizer, he articulated views that helped in important ways to bridge the gap between the libertarians and the traditionalists.

But most important for the emergence of a distinct and coherent conservative movement in the United States have been events. The history of the last two decades has served as the great teacher, both vindicating conservative views and pointing the way to a more integrated conservative world view. The first of these events has a simple name: 1956. That was the year in which Khrushchev described the crimes of Stalin, and the Poles and Hungarians revolted against their workers' paradise. After that no reasonable person could continue to think of the Soviet Union and its socialist society as having any moral standing or any serious claim to be a desirable part of the future. Stalin killed millions, perhaps tens of millions, and for years many liberals refused to believe the evidence. Now they could not escape it. The urban workers, the "proletariat," for whose supposed benefit all this mad slaughter was being carried out, expressed their views of their socialist lives in ways that also could not be ignored.

But it was not enough merely to recognize that the Soviet Union brutally repressed those who came under its control. There was still the need to persuade many Americans that it could happen to them too, if the United States was not willing to prepare itself actively for defense against aggression. But once again the Soviets were able to serve as teachers. The Berlin crisis of 1959–60 and the Cuban missile crisis that effectively ended it showed that both the aggressiveness and the duplicity that the Soviets had already displayed in Hungary and elsewhere would be turned against the United States as soon as they thought they could get away with it. By the end of the Cuban crisis, history had vindicated the anticommunists. Their views became part of the general conservative world view, and penetrated deeply even into liberal and radical consciousness.

A second set of events, much less dramatic but very disturbing to all, has led many to reconsider some traditionalist arguments. In particular this reconsideration has been brought about by the decline of our schools, but also by the rise of crime. Increasingly, we are wondering if these great failures of our society are not connected to the secular and relativistic nature of our socialization of children. As spiritual values come more and more to be things that teachers are forbidden to discuss with their pupils, it is perhaps understandable that the pupils adopt the standards of the streets or of the pop spiritualists of Madison Avenue, the guru business, and rock-star ethics. The abdication of our responsibility to transmit our cultural heritage has perhaps produced these shoddy substitutes, our ravaged and intellectually insipid schools, and the notion that instant gratification is some sort of absolute constitutional right. As parents and taxpayers contemplate the effects of our massive investment in education, it appears to increasing numbers of them that the essence of education, the leading-forth of new lives, is missing from the system. The search for roots is on in earnest once again and, fundamentally, that is the traditionalist's quest.

The third set of events is associated with the failure of liberal policy. The War on Poverty articulated by John Kennedy and put into effect by Lyndon Johnson represented the finest product of the liberals' art, the massive throwing of governmental resources and regulations at a series of identified social "problems." The regulations were put into effect and the money was spent, but, aside from the expenditure, things went on very much as before. There were more bureaucrats, more regulations—and more problems. Even liberals came to recognize that the approach had been a failure, and the minds of millions of citizens were opened by this failure to some of the fundamental arguments libertarian conservatives had been articulating for many years.

By the end of the sixties, events had served in a surprisingly—and distressingly—direct way to vindicate the basic judgments of all three strands of American conservatism. The essential role of property rights and the private market in a free society was now generally recognized by conservatives, as was the need carefully to prepare our defenses against communism, and the need to permit—even encourage—the social processes associated with the preservation and transmission of civilized values. But that is not to say that disagreements among conservatives vanished. Indeed, the fact that such a variety of experiences was generating conservatives, and that so many were relatively recent "converts," suggests that there would be much argument over the specifics of policies and political platforms. This will be true of any active and free association of individuals. And, in fact, much insight as to the nature and future prospects of conservatism can be gained by studying the nature and scope of these differences. In the chapters that follow, we look briefly at some of the most important areas of difference, and, of course, particularly those that impinge on the economy and economic policy. As will be seen, it is now a tale of diversity within the framework of a common central theme.

CHAPTER 17

Libertarians:
The Pure Breed

INDIVIDUALISM is not a crime or a disease. Surely in social theory it represents the highest form of respect for the human being. But radical libertarians have nonetheless been substantially isolated from the mainstream of the conservative movement. In part this is a matter of choice, for their style of argument has tended to be somewhat vociferous. In part it is because of the reaction they have frequently received, which includes outrage and moral opprobrium from the anti-communists and amused contempt from many more orthodox conservatives.

In this chapter we look at a few ideas that come from the more libertarian end of the conservative spectrum. That, in fact, is our first point: This is not a separate wing of conservatism but rather a collection of thinkers whose views vary widely among themselves as to the acceptable role of the state. The reader who finds such views unrealistic may, nevertheless, benefit from them. One of the main functions of extreme arguments is to shake one's mind free of implicit constraints to the serious consideration of certain alternatives. It is quite possible to learn a good deal from radical libertarians without actually becoming one.

James Buchanan is one of the least known of conservative economists outside professional circles, but one of the best known within the economics profession.[1] A specialist on public finance, he has always had a broad perspective on the nature and functions of economic theory as well as having a developed political philosophy. Among his most interesting and useful insights has been his critique of the modern tradition of interpreting market behavior in terms of maximizing or optimizing models. This approach has tended to encourage the manipulators of human behavior, the social engineers. The way in which this works is rather subtle. After all, the models display the market "mechanism" as producing optimal results, which sounds very much like the kind of analysis we were getting in Part I and which is a staple of conservative economics. Who could object to that?

A major problem with the approach is its misplaced precision. Having derived the properties that generate such optimal results, the student finds that, as with all models, there is some considerable idealization of what goes on in the real world built into the assumptions. So next he explores the "deviations" from optimality that result when some of the idealized assumptions are adjusted. But now, in this more realistic world of "imperfect" markets and information and adjustment processes, we find our markets generating "nonoptimal" results; we leave it as an exercise for the reader to determine who is now supposed to return the system to "optimality"! In this way a mode of analysis that looks to be conservative in its implications turns out in practice to be strongly liberal and interventionist.

There are two fundamental criticisms that can be made of this very widely practiced approach of liberal economists. The first is the excess of precision in the specification of the markets' workings. The effect of this is to give the analyst the impression that he has a kind of machine on his hands. To make it run the way he wants it to, he has only to adjust a dial here, twist a valve there, and set the throttle at the efficient point. This kind of thinking by mechanical analogy is what makes Fine Tuners and other similar types of statist economists. That is not what markets are like at all.

The second criticism, and the one emphasized by Buchanan, has to do with the implied criterion by which such markets and market systems are to be manipulated. In order to decide which valves to twist, which government interventions into the market to implement, one must have a criterion by which to contrast the outcomes. Economists call this the "social-welfare function." It is a sort of weighted average of the desires of the individual citizens of the country. Where does it come from? Straight out of the economist's or politician's head. For an individualist there can be no such thing as a social organism; but without some such entity there can be no such thing as a social-welfare function, which purports to represent the desires of society. All it can really do is represent one person's preferences for outcomes. And so the whole idea is senseless—unless one wants to think of the state (the leader?) as representing the true interests of us all.

Buchanan does not simply criticize this mechano-statist approach, he also suggests an alternative mode of market analysis. One should think of markets not as an optimizing device but as a means for resolving conflicts over scarce resources. The essence of this process is deal making, and the heart of deal making is bargaining. There is a presumption that the parties to a voluntarily entered into agreement expect to have their individual lots improved as a result. A whole set of such agreements, which might be called a market, is simply the logical sum of the individual deals. The only known general property of that set is that each deal is expected to make each participant better off. But from an individualist point of view, that is about all that is of interest for the analyst.

Buchanan's suggestion is that game theory is the right way to analyze markets, since the emphasis there is always centered on the payoffs to the individual participants and the process by which they bargain with one another for their individual benefit. It is certainly true that game theory has provided a number of insights into the bargaining process. However, one might reasonably question the productivity and even the promise of this mode of analysis in dealing with social problems. Our optimal conservative of Part I prefers the property-rights format as the appropriate basis for such analysis. This, of course, does not preclude the use of game-theoretic insights where they are relevant. But it does emphasize the structure of rights that exists at the start of any bargaining process, and so serves to focus attention quite naturally on the distinction between outcomes that alter the structure of rights voluntarily and those that do so involuntarily. And that is the heart of the matter when issues of public policy arise.

Buchanan has characterized himself as an anarchist, though a good deal of his writing on public goods economics seems quite ambiguously anarchist in its thrust. No such doubts are generated by a perusal of the works of Murray Rothbard. He represents the pure breed of radical libertarian.[2] For example, he begins a recent book with a proposal simply to abolish even the judiciary apparatus of the state. Instead he claims that as time goes on there will come to be substituted for it a voluntary system of courts. These will be set up by enterprising individuals who sell judicial services to the public. If someone robs you, you identify the culprit to your court for trial. If he has his own hired court and yours and his disagree on the judgment, a system of appellate courts will also arise to adjudicate the differences. Rothbard suggests that there be agreement that the majority decision of two levels of courts prevail; if the culprit is found guilty on appeal, then he will be punished appropriately.

The reader will have a number of questions about this procedure. Presumably the convicted culprit will have to be forcibly brought to punishment. But how to get agreement on this without some agreed-upon instrument of coercion? What if there are two different decisions at the appellate level? If that means the culprit goes free, then surely the market will generate the necessary courts to provide this service, for a fee, to criminals. And how can you get individuals to testify voluntarily, when it is not in their interest? By paying them? The questions go on, and Rothbard does not bother to answer any of them.

However, the reader who stops reading Rothbard at this early point will have made a mistake. When he turns from the functions of the state associated with the preservation of order to those associated with the control of markets, Rothbard begins to make a good deal more sense. His views are those of an anarchist; they are extreme. But they are also salutary, for even libertarians at times have unquestioningly accepted a role for the state that may not stand up to scrutiny.

We may take as an example of this latter tendency a recent work by Robert Posner that attempts to use economic criteria, and particularly the notion of efficiency, as a basis for appraising the working of the law.[3] One of his most interesting findings is that in a wide variety of cases the best defense of rules of law lies not in their justice but in their promotion of efficient outcomes. For example, if you bring me to court for having done you some wrong, the issue of justice really has to do only with our particular case, with whether I in fact should be held responsible for any harm you suffered. But from the point of view of the law as an effective social institution, Posner argues, the real issue is the effect of the decision on future actions of individuals. And this suggests strongly that the court will be much concerned with finding a decision that will promote the most efficient behavior by individuals who fall into a similar situation in the future. Even if I am not really morally responsible for the harm done, if it is much cheaper and more convenient for me to take preventive actions, the court may well be justified in finding against me.

This approach to the defense of legal rules has a great deal of promise. In particular, it seems to cut through the "judicial rhetoric," as Posner calls it, that often obscures the real reasoning behind judicial decisions. However, in the case of contract law, there appear to be several instances where Posner's analysis is flawed. It is as if he had gotten a bit carried away with the idea of defending existing rules, and had forgotten that he is also supposed to appraise them. Perhaps this has generally been true of conservatives, who have not seriously considered whether the entire body of contract law actually is necessary in a free society.

The basic issue that is posed by the efficiency approach is: To what extent are we willing to accept coercion in order to improve economic efficiency? Rothbard's answer would be straightforward—one should never accept such a tradeoff, no matter how great the improvement in efficiency. A more moderate and traditional conservative position might run as follows: You have mistaken the basic issue. Law is one of our most powerful institutions just because it represents the distillation and codification of a hundred generations of experience with human conflict. One should remember that historically the primary motivation for the state's coercive intervention in private affairs was the preservation of order. Contracts are enforced because conflicts over contract violations have been a frequent source of disorder and violence in past societies. If you agree to build me a house for a fee and I refuse to pay, hoping to retain both the house and my money, you have a strong motivation to do something about it. If the law won't help, there is some reasonable prospect of your taking matters into your own hands. Law, even contract law, interposed the state between two such parties in the interest of preserving order.

This defense of the law of contract seems much more reasonable than the efficiency defense. But it is now reasonable to ask whether the law has not gone too far in the scope of its interpositions between the disputing parties. There is some evidence that this is the case. As judicial dockets have become more crowded and the cost of litigation has increased, the tendency to resolve contract disputes by private arbitration has grown until nowadays the number of cases settled by the latter method is at least an order of magnitude greater than the number settled by the former method. The parties to the settlement have good reason to accept it; they are engaged in continual contract making and so their reputation for honesty and fair dealing is worth a good deal of money to them. Without that reputation, potential partners in deals will surely go elsewhere. This suggests that much of the efficiency gain from having contracts enforced may be achievable without the need for coercive interposition of the state.

This point about contract law is not being made because the law seems to be overly coercive in any fundamental sense. Instead the aims are two: first, to suggest that the radical libertarian questions can often be profitably asked by a conservative who accepts many functions for the state; and second, because an attitude based essentially on an attempt to rationalize the law in economic terms misses a rather fundamental point. If contract law is in not too bad shape, the same definitely cannot be said of the massive and rapidly growing body of administrative law. This latter poses threats to freedom both in its directly destructive impact on private property rights and in its more insidious effects in promoting the further dominance of the modern leviathan. To analyze administrative laws, one after another, in order to test them against an efficiency criterion makes a mockery of the conservative analysis of law. The general formula should be: While recognizing law's deep roots in human experience, no segment of the law should be immune from critical appraisal as to the reality of the claimed need for coercive intervention into human affairs.

The most original and stimulating work of political philosophy to appear in recent years is Robert Nozick's *Anarchy, State, and Utopia.*[4] Nozick argues that the nightwatchman or minimal state, the one in which the state is essentially limited to protecting its citizens against violence, theft, and fraud, would arise naturally out of a state of anarchy. That is to say, if we were to start from a situation in which there was no legitimate coercive power, we could reasonably decide to move from that state to the minimal state without imposing solutions on any who would not be prepared to harm others for personal gain. More important, Nozick claims, using a variety of ingenious arguments, we would not be able to move any farther than the minimal state in expanding state powers without being forced to impose our will on some reluctant minorities. Since we have all grown accustomed to the liberal style of argument in these matters, reading Nozick comes as something of a shock. But clearly, this is a line of argument that every thinking citizen should have the opportunity to appraise for himself.

We may take just two of Nozick's points to illustrate the relevance of his work. The first is a notion of justice in social arrangements. That situation is just, he argues, which has been reached by processes that do not involve violation of anyone's rights. At each point

in time each individual has a set of entitlements, essentially rights that
he has acquired. Only those future situations can be considered just
that preserve the entitlements that exist in today's situation. Private
agreements preserve entitlements, given the absence of fraud. Government action designed to protect and preserve entitlements is justified. Nothing else is. Clearly, we have here an argument from political
philosophy that matches the spirit and essence of the arguments about
markets and property rights that have occupied so much of the attention of conservative economists. And, in fact, a conservative economist
feels quite comfortable, intellectually speaking, as he works his way
through Nozick's book.

Now consider as an application of the above argument the contrast
between two theories of redistribution. Most arguments in favor of the
redistribution of income or assets have some sort of conception of an
ideal pattern of distribution as it should exist at any one point in time.
At one extreme is the pure egalitarian, who wants all incomes to be
equal. Liberals generally accept inequality that compensates for onerous employment or, to some extent, that provides incentives to up-
grade skills. But you will often find them saying things such as: "There
is no reason why the ratio of the highest to the lowest income in
society should exceed six or seven." That specifies a pattern. And
patterns are just what it is not possible to justify, according to Nozick.
He argues against patterning but for a historical interpretation of the
just income distribution. For that is what his entitlements theory does.
The current distribution of income or assets over the population is of
no interest whatsoever; that is, it gives us no usable information as to
whether the current distribution in just. Instead, we must look to the
process by which the income was acquired. Once again, if it was acquired through legitimate processes that did not infringe the rights
of others, then the current distribution, whatever its pattern, is justified.
Not outcomes but moral behavior is the desideratum; and surely that
is a morally satisfying rule.

In sum, the libertarians have and will continue to play an important role in conservatism. The very vigor with which they defend their
views is a good part of their strength, for they force a thinking
through of positions that all too often have been conceded by default
to liberals. Often they seem to go too far. In an important sense there
can be no such thing as a radical conservative, for the seeking out
and nurturing and transmitting of all that is valuable in our heritage
must be at the center of any conservative philosophy. But clearly, a
major problem for the preservation of a free society is to turn government around, and move it step by step back toward a more appropriate
role, paying due attention to the protection of existing property rights
in the process. In that process even the strictest libertarians are both
allies and colleagues in the conservative cause.[5]

CHAPTER 18

Social Conservatives

IN a closing note to his great work, *The Constitution of Liberty*, Friedrich Hayek lists three criticisms of traditional conservatism that serve to explain why he does not consider himself to fit under that label: Conservatives fear and resist all change, they are too fond of authority, and they do not understand economic forces. I suppose no one would want to join such a group. Our job in this chapter is to see whether those charges are justifiable when applied to some contemporary versions of the more traditional brand of conservatism.

In dealing with conservatism in the traditional sense, the first thing to talk about is civilization.[1] A nation, in the old sense of that word, takes its essence from the cultural values that are held and passed on through a leading stratum of the society. There are only a small number of distinct civilizations in the world, Judeo-Christian civilization representing one of these, Chinese civilization another. Each such civilization, of course, has a number of variants, conditioned by localisms of various kinds, and each tradition undergoes change as it moves through the generations. But it is also coherent and in fundamental ways recognizably the same distinct entity despite these variations.

At the heart of every civilization, every developed and city-based traditional culture, is a concept of order. Civilization is impossible without a large measure of order, which in every case means a recognition that others are not to be disturbed in the exercise of their rights. What the particular concept of order does is spell out the things that for that civilization may be considered rights.

At the heart of the Judeo-Christian sense of order is the concept of the rule of law. The idea of the rule of law has, in innumerable situations in the history of the Western world, been a force that interposed itself between ruler and subject, forcing the former to recognize some right of the latter to be free of harassment. The law has, of course, grown out of several sources. Much of family and tort law may be a product of attempts by the ruler to impose order in the most direct sense of preventing private wars. Much of contract law derives from the medieval Law Merchant, which grew out of practical trading activities and whose enforcement by the state was only undertaken rather late. But the idea of a state-based but quasi-autonomous arbiter of justice is uniquely central to our civilization, and it goes far to explain why our civilization is the one that, more than any others, has fostered the idea of the society of liberty.[2]

This central concept has had a variety of other influences on our civilization. The idea of the rule of law tends to encourage rational deliberative thought and choice, for it is only through rational debate of the merits of a case, and deliberative weighing of the evidence, that reasonable choices can be made and justice done. Furthermore, distinctive ideas as to the nature of moral behavior are fostered by this deeply rooted cultural value and institution. The law codifies, summarizes, and defends the joint products of a hundred generations of weighing evidence and appraising the relative merits, in situations involving immediate human conflict, of alternative rules of law as the appropriate rule of justice. This great freight of moral wisdom has permeated the civilization and lent specific tone and character to ideas of morality.

We have been discussing only one aspect of civilization and its impact; of course there are many others. But perhaps the point has been made: There is much of direct contemporary relevance built into our traditions, which in turn are passed on, through the great cultural works of our civilization, from one generation to the next. A central requirement if we are to continue to survive and thrive is that we do preserve and spread and hand down that tradition, for if we do not much that has held our society together in the past will be lost. And surely there is no doubt but that America is a part of the Judeo-Christian civilized tradition.

Apparently not all conservatives would find the above remarks acceptable. Frank Knight, one of the founders of the Chicago School, has argued that the Judeo-Christian religion is in some respects contradictory to liberalism—what these days we call libertarianism—and does not offer moral insights of value in our rapidly changing world. Others might fear that such language opens the door to reestablishing Christianity as a state religion. And the more rationalistic among conservative thinkers seem to be almost indifferent to history as a source of contemporary understanding. Clearly, there is a substantive area of difference among conservatives in this regard.

Nevertheless, I think the extent of disagreement is much exaggerated, especially in those critical remarks of Hayek with which this chapter began. Perhaps the best way to make this point is by surveying very briefly some of Joseph Schumpeter's ideas. Here we have an economist who, though dead now for a quarter of a century, has left a strong imprint on economics that continues to influence even some young technicians. Schumpeter was a conservative; he thought of himself as one and was widely regarded as one. His most fundamental contribution to economics was the development of a sort of messy dynamics, a sense of the laws of motion of the capitalist system that took full account of the human and the unpredictable in their course. At the center of the process of change for Schumpeter was the entrepreneur, the person who sees an opportunity to break the chains of tradition by introducing new methods of production or of organizing production. The dynamics of the capitalist system were for Schumpeter largely a product of the system of private property rights, which put fewer obstacles in the way of such men's activities.

Of course, society put some obstacles in their way. Clearly, inertia and resistance to change are central survival values, essential to the preservation of any kind of order. The key to the rise of the modern world has been the striking of an appropriate balance between resistance to change and more or less graceful acceptance of it. But there is more of the conservative in Schumpeter than this. Essentially, his entrepreneurs are "breaking chains" for conservative purposes. They want to found dynasties, to promote not only their personal interests but also those of their families. Knight once said that free societies might more reasonably be called "familistic" than individualistic; that too is an exaggeration, but it captures the central notions of social cohesion and drive that operate in Schumpeter's interpretation of dynamic capitalism. Obviously, the success of such a vibrant society requires not only restraint but adaptation on the part of conservative forces

To this idea of more or less controlled change Schumpeter added an idea of democracy. He notes that in successful democracies leadership tends to come from a relatively limited stratum of society. In these people's hands lies the understanding of the processes of government, the ability to rule. What the people do in a democracy is choose from among the members of this stratum who compete in elections for their favor: They choose often not even a specific leader, but a government. Such a government can only carry out its tasks successfully if it has a rather limited number of tasks to perform. The leadership must spend part of its time competing for reelection, and the process of negotiating and implementing laws takes much time. Only if these conditions are met can democracy function successfully.

This view combines much of the heart of both libertarian and traditional conservatism. Tradition supplies and instructs the leading stratum of political leaders and sets up a flexible but systematic system of barriers to change. Private property rights provide freedom for entrepreneurial maneuver. Family provides social cohesion, a vehicle for the passing on of tradition, and a central incentive for work and change and conservation all at once. And limited government provides flexibility, some measure of efficiency, and the prospect of preservation of rights.

This summary does great damage to the richness and power of Schumpeter's thought. However, our aim was very modest, being only to suggest that here, embodied in Schumpeter's works, we find a cogent answer to the charge that traditional and libertarian conservatives have little in common. Schumpeter certainly understood economic forces as well as anyone has. He did not fear change, and he gives a meaning to the idea of resistance to change that makes it an intelligible and necessary component of the healthy society. And there seems little doubt that, whatever the extent of his "fondness" for authority, he was fully aware of both the nature and the desirable properties of democracy. While thus failing all of Hayek's tests for a traditional conservative, he nonetheless seems deeply rooted in that tradition in his own thought and analysis.

However, there is one place where perhaps differences between libertarians and traditionalists *are* reflected by Schumpeter. Schumpeter, like many traditionalists, was a pessimist who believed that the modern world was moving inevitably away from democracy and toward a social structure that would be excessively resistant to entrepreneurial efforts. Culture, the intellectuals, were being mobilized against capitalism, organized interests were forcing rapidly increasing activities on government, and bureaucracies were stifling individual initiative. In Schumpeter's system the result was wholly predictable, namely, the replacement of capitalism by some bureaucratic alternative, probably socialism.

That process has been continuing, except that private "bureaucracies" seem to have developed in a much more flexible and creative way than Schumpeter expected. But the continued movement of government in a direction that is inconsistent with the preservation of democracy is clear enough, certainly to conservatives of all kinds. Suppose the tide is not stemmed, and we pass the point of no return in which democracy's days are clearly numbered. What then? Would traditional conservatives begin to think in terms of the "second best," that is, of trying to see that that next, inevitably nondemocratic form of government, be as good as possible? If so, they will find some guidance in their tradition, which seems clearly to favor oligarchy among the nondemocratic alternatives. And perhaps the experience of the Venetian republic has some hints to offer as to the great danger to be avoided, namely, tyranny or dictatorship or communism. But the libertarian cannot reasonably follow his fellow conservative down this path. His commitment to freedom would seem to permit no discussion of a political second best, no contingency plans against the failure of democracy. If this *is* a difference, it is clearly a fundamental one.

The so-called Wallaceites constitute a group that has often been called conservative, and whose rallying to the conservative banner has been advocated occasionally by political spokesmen for conservatism. Perhaps the relationship between our optimal Part I conservatism and the problems associated with this group can serve to distinguish some relevant issues of social conservatism. In the first place, it is clear that a good many individuals who are not among America's wealthy subscribe to conservative principles. We were once a thoroughgoing market economy; the ideals of self-help, individualism, and individual responsibility were once taught as central values of our culture. There are still a great many millions of Americans around who subscribe to those values and will vote for candidates for political office who advocate them publicly.

There are both good and bad reasons for thinking of former supporters of George Wallace as potential recruits to conservatism. Many of them are troubled by the deterioration of their neighborhoods, many by rising crime, many by the continued and even escalating bureaucratic hassling of small business, which for all too many has become a survival issue. In all these cases conservatism has an answer. The protection of civil and property rights of law-abiding citizens as a central concern, the drastic cutback of government regulation, the drastic reduction in federal funds available for "urban renewal," the shifting of basic responsibility for many aspects of government, and particularly of schooling, back to the local and even neighborhood level: These are all part of the core program of a contemporary American conservative.

However, there are two areas where conservatives and Wallace-ites must part company. In the first place, there is a substantial component of old-fashioned populism in the movement, and populism has been intimately associated with dramatic expansions of government intervention in the economy. And second, there has been a strong vein of racism running through the movement. On the political side there are still conservatives willing to use racism in order to get votes, and they have tended to give a tone of racism to the movement. There is no way such ideas can be reconciled with the idea of a free society; furthermore, such tactics have tended to put off many who might on grounds of principle be attracted to political conservatism. Much the same thing is true of any sort of implicit appeals for the latent populist vote, including such things as ticket-balancing with liberals. Over the longer run, which is surely the run that counts for conservatives, there must be a basic compatibility between the principles of conservatism and the practice of conservative politicians; otherwise, it is all too easy to dismiss the movement as an unprincipled front for the material interests of the wealthy.

There is an area of legitimate disagreement between libertarian and traditional conservatives. Much of it hinges in practice on the extent to which the requirements of preserving a regime of order must constrain the requirements of preserving a regime of liberty. Reasonable men can differ on such matters. But perhaps enough has been said in this chapter to convince doubting libertarian conservatives that traditional conservatives are a bit more sophisticated than Hayek gives them credit for being. And hopefully our optimal conservative position of Part I will convince both groups that their mutual interests are far geater than their disagreements, that they are, in fact, all conservatives.

CHAPTER 19

Neoconservatives

"HOW DOES a radical, a mild radical, it is true, but still one who felt closer to radical than to liberal writers and politicians in the late nineteen fifties, end up a conservative, a mild conservative, but still closer to those who call themselves conservative than to those who call themselves liberal in early nineteen seventy?" With this question Harvard sociologist Nathan Glazer introduces us to the neoconservatives. They are a fascinating phenomenon, as much for their eminence as for their numbers. They indicate in an intellectually very powerful way that conservatism is passing its current tests of relevance and plausibility with flying colors. Conservatism is gaining recruits from the hitherto dominant liberals, and among its recruits are those who have been centrally involved in creating and appraising the liberal handiwork of the preceding two decades. It seems they have come to think it doesn't work.[1]

Neoconservatives are not the same thing as conservatives. Perhaps they can most easily be distinguished from optimal conservatives by the following three tests. Conservatives tend to believe three things about public policies for the improvement of the citizenry: (1) manipulation, especially coercive manipulation by government of some people by others, is a fundamentally immoral activity. (2) We know very little about the consequences for human behavior of any given policy, which inserts a large area of unpredictability into such manipulations. (3) Even if the "productivity" of a particular public policy is known, its real effects are not because of the fundamental inefficiency of bureaucratic government, its inability effectively to implement policy.

On my reading, neoconservatives tend to reject point 1 above, and their conservatism rests more on point 2 than on point 3. In other words, neoconservatives are basically liberals who have become disillusioned by the failures of public policy, failures that they attribute in large part to their—and, of course, our—ignorance. To this they might want to add an additional point: (4) What we are learning about such basic problems as crime, welfare, and the functioning of urban communities suggests that we have very little public policy leverage in changing urban behavior and ways of life. The knowledge accumulated over the past ten or fifteen years seems to be telling us more about what we cannot do in the way of public policy than about what we can do. Conservatives might partly disagree on this one, arguing that public policy does have considerable power to do evil, but I doubt that there would be much disagreement from anyone on the latter point nowadays. The neoconservative, of course, is talking about our knowledge of how to make things better.

In other words, neoconservatives seem basically to retain their liberal orientation. Their alliance with conservatives is based on disillusion rather than conversion. If a way could be found to design effective liberal policies, they would come flocking back to the banner. At any rate they *are* allies, for the moment, and the reasons may be worth taking a closer look at. Just a few points about city life will be noted to give the flavor of their orientation.

1. Standard fare of liberal argumentation decries the "flight to the suburbs" as something new and very disturbing in American urban life, a sort of renouncing of responsibility by the citizenry for making cities work. But it turns out that in fact this is nothing new, that the "flight" has been going on for a century and more in our older cities. Such a movement by the increasingly affluent has occurred regularly with the growth of cities, which has meant crowding and increasing land values near the center. The more affluent want space and privacy, and can afford the move; developing modes of transportation have made the commute substantially less onerous. Far from being a new and fundamental social problem, it is part of a standard pattern of urban growth.

2. However, something new was added, mostly in the post–World War II environment. This was a change in central city job structure combined with the introduction of substantially higher welfare payments to the poor in many urban areas. The new jobs tended to be white-collar and service-sector jobs, mostly for the middle class, instead of following the older pattern of industries using cheap semi-skilled labor. So appropriate new job opportunities failed to keep up. But the increased welfare payments kept the supply of newly migrant lower-class families to the city up, or even accelerated it. The result, substantially a product of well-intentioned public policy, was to turn our central city areas into a sort of adult "sandbox" where welfare recipients were congregated and were actually encouraged by public policy to give up their sense of responsibility and live as government charges. Out of this mistaken policy, substantially reinforcing an underlying change in urban job structure, has come the major causal element in deteriorating neighborhoods and crime.

3. One fundamental variable serves quite well to distinguish members of different social strata. This variable is the degree of present orientation or, to put it another way, the degree to which an individual is willing to defer present gratification in order to have a more affluent or secure future. The lower class, the bottom 10 to 20 percent in the American status and income pyramid, display extreme

present orientation in their behavior. What happens, then, when policies are applied that are designed to jump status, to pull members of the lower class up into the middle class in their behavior? Of course, they will fail. For a striking example, there was the attempt in the later sixties to get the poor to organize their neighborhoods for political action. Funds were made available as an incentive to participate, and the poor were thus shown the way, the blessings of participation in the democratic process. Had this been tried in an upper middle-class neighborhood, it would no doubt have been a great success. But turnouts were abysmally low in poor neighborhoods. And all too often the funds became the stakes of what looked like developing old-style precinct political machines, with all the corruption and coercion that entailed.[2]

4. It seems quite likely that the minimum-wage law, another well-intentioned attempt to prevent "exploitation," has the opposite effect from that intended. There is quite good reason to believe that raising the minimum wage reduces the number of people employers are willing to hire. Since the minimum-wage law will mostly affect entry-level job seekers, this employment effect is largely concentrated on teen-agers. And since they mostly live in families where they are not the only source of income, on the average the effects of lower wages on them should not be too severe. So what *does* happen when the minimum wage is instituted or raised? Probably there is a higher level of teen-age unemployment. That is a bad thing in itself, but indirectly it may contribute significantly to the crime rate, since teen-agers commit most of the crimes, particularly the street crimes.

5. Not all policies have the opposite effect from that intended by liberal policymakers. Probably most of them have some net beneficial effect. However, a survey of individual policies in the areas of housing, health, and education, specifically as they relate to blacks, indicates that individual policy effects, where they can be discerned at all, tend to be relatively trivial in the net benefits they generated. And, of course, they tend to be rather more than trivial in the net costs they incur.

6. Finally, one might mention the great overall panacea of the liberal economist, namely, monetary and fiscal policy. The textbooks used to say that a proper application of these twin public policy instruments could keep the economy growing at or very near full employment. No more. It does not take a professional economist to see that these instruments are not working very well, that something has gone wrong with the economist's ability to predict the consequences for prices and employment of Keynesian-type economic stimulus. Controversy is even emerging among liberal economists as to the appropriate direction of change, as in arguments over whether we would have had more or less inflation by adopting expansionary policies after the OPEC price rise.

This is an interesting and powerful line of argument. The list could certainly be extended. But it should be noted that for conservatives these points represent ammunition, specific confirmations of conservative views of the consequences of adopting the liberal relation of government to the individual. They do not represent new principles, or even basically new ideas. A conservative who believes in freedom and understands the social benefits of tradition would naturally gravitate in these directions, even without the help of the more specific studies that convinced these neoconservatives.

There is, however, an additional thread to neoconservatism. It is espoused by sociologists rather than economists, but is worth mentioning here because it represents a widespread misunderstanding of the basis of American conservatism. The argument might run something like this: There are two ways to look at the law. The first is to think of it as a sort of tied sale. Most of us, following the intent of the law, do not think we have become criminals because we have gotten, and earned, a parking ticket. Many will make a sort of rational cost-benefit calculation; if it's worth the risk of a four-dollar fine, we go ahead and park in the prohibited zone. But some, perhaps an increasing number of citizens, carry this idea over into the realm of genuinely criminal activities such as theft and even murder. If this becomes the general reaction of the population to laws, the lawmaker and the judicial system must then design and implement the law as if it were a sort of cost-benefit system. A good legal system would then be one in which potential criminals assess the costs and benefits of crime and find that crime really does not pay.

A second view of law gives it moral authority. Legitimacy is the word political scientists use; the population by and large does not stop to weigh the costs and benefits of a crime, but genuinely believes that to commit a crime is an immoral act. Only when laws are legitimated, proponents of this view argue, does the judicial system have a manageable task. Legitimacy means that simply announcing a law will have a negative effect on criminal behavior; and that is the decisive edge for a society of order.

Which view is right? In answering that question, one might remember the third point above. The more present-oriented individual is much more likely to commit a crime if he sees an immediate opportunity for gain. However, he is quite unlikely to make a careful calculation of the overall and longer term costs and benefits of the act. His behavior—and probably most criminals fall into the lower or present-oriented class on this characterization—can only be controlled by making sure that the costs are large and occur in the short run. And much of the effectiveness of the judicial system will stem simply from successfully getting such people off the streets for a reasonable period after they have committed a crime. Swift and sure punishment, not some abstract distinction between legitimacy and rationalism, is the major issue here. And so the issue does not divide conservatives in any fundamental sense. Both ideas have their place.

Surely it would be pleasant if all citizens respected the law, and we should endeavor to expose our citizens to the many good arguments in favor of doing so. And equally surely neither the government in general, nor the judicial system in particular, is capable of generating a highly "productive" set of instruments as inputs to the individual decision to commit or not to commit the crime. That part leads right back to liberalism and the issues with which we started. But clearly, there are a number of areas where simple improvements in procedure, sentencing, and parole, combined with eliminating the encouragement to crime of much other social policy, could have a dramatic effect on this and other current social problems. The valid element in the search for legitimacy is contained in the conservative concept of order as the precondition of freedom.

CHAPTER 20

Friedman

WITHOUT A DOUBT Milton Friedman is America's best-known conservative economist. He has gained this renown through his regular articles in *Newsweek* over the years and through the publicized advice he has given to politicians. But Friedman is far more than a public pundit. He has done a number of solid and scholarly studies in the economics of public policy and is recognized as a leading professional by his colleagues. If the honors he received as he moved to emeritus status had not matched those of other leading economists, it would have reflected not on Friedman but on the profession itself.[1]

Nevertheless, Friedman has not escaped criticism even from within the conservative, libertarian camp. It is true that he has not pursued the philosophical interests that engaged the previous generation of conservative scholars such as Hayek and Mises and Friedman's own teacher at Chicago, Frank Knight. He has done no serious work on political philosophy or the nature of man, and has renounced Knight's profound if eclectic view of science for a rather rigid positivism. And some have found in his various policy proposals a sort of gimmickry that seemed to them inconsistent with the conservative view that human social arrangements are not lightly to be disturbed. In combination, this set of qualities in his writing could lead to the claim that Friedman is something of a radical, whose schemes for reform are at once too drastic and too simplistic to be truly conservative and truly useful. It is this criticism primarily that we appraise in the present chapter.

As an initial example of Friedman at work, we may recall the issue of fixed versus floating exchange rates in international finance, which was discussed in chapter 12. In 1962 Friedman published a list of seven steps that should be taken to free up the international monetary mechanism, of which the switch to floating exchange rates was the key step. Most liberal economists opposed these moves, but a decade later they had all been taken, and after a half dozen years of living with floating rates we seem to be surviving quite nicely, especially considering the disturbances OPEC and other agents have inflicted on world markets.

Friedman has done a little crowing over these events, which he is certainly entitled to do. But he has also carefully noted that he himself was not the principal agent of change in the matter. Liberal economists were not convinced by his arguments during the sixties— though many of them have been persuaded by now. Instead, politicians were forced by events to switch to the more robust system. Consequently, the gimmickry charge can hardly be sustained in this case. The approach called for reducing government involvement in markets, and it was chosen by the politicians because it seemed that there was no alternative. In that context the only charge one could reasonably level at Friedman is the free exercise of common sense.

As a second example, we may consider Friedman's discussion of social security. He divides the issue into three parts: the redistribution of income entailed by the system, the nationalization of the system for the provision of the pensions, and the compulsory "purchase" of the pension-annuity by almost all citizens. The redistributions go in two directions, from younger entrants into the system to older entrants, and from general taxpayers to recipients of pensions. Neither is very easy to justify, even if one were willing to impose one of the more popular egalitarian notions of equity onto the issue. Nationalization of the annuity means that the money paid by working people into the system goes through the government budget, and the terms and organization of the system are under full government ownership and control. This despite the fact that we have in the United States a large and competitive insurance industry, which would be fully competent to provide the service on a private basis for a fee and which would keep the pressure on for efficient delivery of the service. Also, requiring people to join the system seems to be based mainly on a depression-bred misconception that people could not take care of themselves in their old age through planned saving during their working years.

We will make no attempt to appraise Friedman's arguments here, except to note that all of them have some force and all of them are of even more significance today than they were fifteen years ago, when they were first published. In particular, we are now approaching the time when a very substantial redistribution of income from current taxpayers to pension recipients will be occurring every year, while the vagaries of the various other pension plans, when combined with social security, are putting a very heavy burden on a number of budgets, including those of city governments. It might also be noted that the rise in the federal social-security budget may have played a stimulating role in the rise of other government expenditures, particularly during the years in which social security was running a substantial surplus of receipts over pension payments.

But once again it is hard to find a basis for accusing Friedman of gimmickry or of simplistic radical reformism. In this case the issue is separated into three distinct parts. One could without great difficulty devise a policy that would deal with only one of these parts, so that reform need not occur in one fell swoop. Furthermore, Friedman's implied proposals in each of the three areas are consistent with overall conservative principles. And, as with exchange rates, time seems to have made his case more cogent, not less. Once again, from our present standpoint his position looks more like common sense than anything else.

The three areas where the gimmickry charge seems to be most persistent are the negative income tax proposal, the proposed abolition of licenses to practice skills and professions, and the proposal to substitute educational vouchers for the tax-supported public school system. Each of these represents quite a dramatic change from the current situation, none is based on traditional practice, and there are some reasonable objections to feasibility that a conservative might legitimately raise. But once again, each proposal probably looks better today than it did fifteen years ago, and each has been an important issue of public policy in the intervening years.

As Friedman points out, probably the most difficult aspect of these issues stems from the extent to which any government policy is based on paternalism. The less one is willing to trust the judgment of those who receive the benefits, or their customers in the case of licensure, the less attractive are Friedman's proposals. Paternalism is a difficult question to appraise in Friedmanian terms. Part of the problem is that the libertarian's notion of social arrangements is based on trust of the individual, combined with a desire to foster that trust by making the individual responsible for the consequences of his own actions. But the negative income tax is not much better than the handout in kind in this respect: In each case, the individual becomes a ward of the state. With educational vouchers the parent is given a voucher worth the regular per-pupil allocation for public school operation for each of his children and is then allowed to send the child to the school of his choice, paying the cost with the voucher. But this too involves paternalism in a most direct way, since the child is not being given responsibility for the decision. The paternalism in licensure comes from the claim that the customer, such as a doctor's patient, is in no position to judge the quality of the service before it is administered, and so must be helped by the state. So really in all of these cases the extent to which government paternalism is required becomes a central issue.

Probably all conservatives can agree that expenditures are excessive as compared to results in the case of both welfare and education. It also seems likely that Friedman's proposals will have some beneficial effect on the cost of these services. But that is by no means a necessary outcome. One could easily think of tax and voucher rates being set at levels that far outstrip current levels of payment. This absence of built-in checks to further expansion of the government system is clearly a troubling aspect of each proposal. When combined with the reduction in the government's ability to control outcomes in areas in which it provides the money, a feature of both proposals, there is further reason for conservative doubts. For example, are tax-subsidized children to be exposed to any political and social views in the schools of their parents' choice? Is any use of the welfare funds by parents to be accepted? Would it not be better to concentrate efforts on reducing the scope and size of the present program by weeding out obvious fraud and mismanagement than on substituting an entirely different program whose size is easily varied to suit the desires of politicians?

Licensure raises somewhat similar issues. It is true that there has been much abuse of licensing and that it has often resulted in establishing a government-licensed trade union that keeps prices up by restricting entry. But there also seems to be a reasonable sense in which such systems, for example in medicine, have served to keep the general quality of medical practice quite high. Our current health-care system is criticized on many grounds, but rarely if ever on grounds of the general incompetence of physicians. Once again it might seem more reasonable to concentrate on the obvious failures of the system, many of which stem from the peculiar attempts at a mixture of public and private systems of service, rather than on the fact that doctors and nurses have to work hard to obtain licenses to practice. If the government were to concentrate its efforts on that area in which it has a clear obligation to act, namely, in the field of public health, and were to leave the art of healing to the combined efforts of the existing market mechanisms and private organizations, the health status of the American population might be substantially better. But it does not seem that licensure is particularly relevant to these more central issues.

This is not to say that Friedman's ideas are to be rejected out of hand. Rather, it is to suggest that there are reasonable and conservative arguments on the other side, and that this is perhaps an area in which the conservative position is in need of clarification by further research. No one can reasonably deny that Friedman has raised important issues, and has pointed to important areas of failure of our current social arrangements. And no conservative can reasonably appraise these areas without giving careful attention to Friedman's proposals.

There is one peculiar area of neglect in much of Friedman's work. This is his lack of use of the property rights framework in his analyses. Friedman's approach to a problem is to look at what the reasonable aims of public policy may be, then to look at the results of government action, and finally to ask how things would be if the government were to do things differently, in particular if government were forced to rely more on rules and less on discretion in its behavior. There is a clear connection between a government based on rules and the stability of a structure of private property rights. The more discretion government has, the more uncertain is the definition of the property rights of those who fall within government's purview. But that is not to say that Friedman's approach is equivalent to the property-rights approach. Government discretion may itself be limited, for example to those whose failure to function effectively in the marketplace brings them under the paternalistic wing of the welfare program. It is by no means clear that one wants to establish private property rights to the receipt of welfare largesse. Discretion in this area may, in fact, do more good than harm by decentralizing some aspects of decision making. Whether it will or not is a question of fact. But conservatives can reasonably object to the insistence on granting to the citizenry property rights to enjoy either welfare or a job. If the government is going to be paternalistic in certain areas, there is a good case for allowing it some flexibility, within the budget, in deciding where and how to act. Perhaps systematic consideration of Friedman's proposals within a property-rights framework will serve to provide the needed clarification.

One of the most striking things about the set of proposals Friedman has put forward is their mutual coherence. Each one seems to come from the same basic social orientation, and they are typically not only mutually compatible but mutually reinforcing. In combination they provide a vision of a thoroughgoing market economy functioning successfully in the twentieth century. That is a vision that conservatives badly needed fifteen or twenty years ago. And there is no question but that it is a serious vision and not some half-baked utopia. I remember in the early sixties a one-liner that was going the rounds of economists: "Friedman loses all the arguments—except for the ones at which he is actually present!" This reflected a typical liberal reaction to his work; Friedman's views were never really taken seriously, and so they were not accurately reproduced or fairly appraised by liberal economists. But when he presented them himself, the audience tended to come away from the talk in a thoughtful mood. That thinking has proved to be very subversive of the liberal values of the sixties. Even if some of the specifics of Friedman's proposals are rejected by conservatives, he is deserving of their respect and gratitude for the subversive power of his thought.

Hayek

OF ALL contemporary conservative writers, it is Friedrich Hayek who comes closest to the positions of our optimal conservative economic world view. Such differences as do exist are essentially matters of emphasis and style, and of the desire for simplicity in the Part I presentation. However, Hayek is often misunderstood, or at least misinterpreted. Perhaps that is a burden all profound and subtle minds must bear. In the present chapter we offer a few quotes and comments from Hayek's principal works. Our aim is to suggest to the reader for whom this is a first contact with Hayek that his rather heavy tomes may well repay the effort they require. But we also hope to show that Hayek's more philosophical and historical approach to problems does in fact tend in the same direction as do the more mundane arguments of our optimal conservative economist.

1. Consider first this quote from *The Constitution of Liberty:* "Far from assuming that those who created the institutions were wiser than we are, the evolutionary view is based on the insight that the result of the experimentation of many generations may embody more experience than any one man possesses." [1] Hayek thus identifies himself with a respect for tradition and against the rationalist apotheosis of reason. But again: "To the empiricist evolutionary tradition, on the other hand, the value of freedom consists mainly in the opportunity it provides for the growth of the undesigned, and the beneficial functioning of a free society rests largely on the existence of such freely grown institutions." [2] Thus the mixture of freedom and tradition, and the emphasis on the emergence through trial and error of a complex product that far transcends the reasoning abilities of Man the Planner.

2. In chapter 19 there was some discussion of the emphasis placed especially by Irving Kristol on the need for a set of shared values if society is not to fly apart. As Hayek puts it: ". . . freedom has never worked without deeply ingrained moral beliefs and that coercion can be reduced to a minimum only where individuals can be expected as a rule to conform voluntarily to certain principles." [3] But Hayek would not go so far as to attempt to coerce the acceptance of moral

rules; by implication he would rather see less order and so, indirectly, less freedom in other spheres. He also notes that, in fact, it is at times desirable for some generally held moral rules to be broken, for they too are not forever fixed, provided the breaker is prepared to assume the consequences of his act. This passage might have provided good counsel to many who, a few years after it was written, had to face the moral dilemmas of the middle and late sixties.

3. There is an important distinction, Hayek notes, between the situation of the giver and the taker of employment. The worker's responsibility is restricted to the performance of assigned tasks, while the giver of employment bears a general and open-ended responsibility for the success of the entire venture. Most people seem to prefer that restricted responsibility. The job and the income are relatively secure most of the time. As a result the worker tends to forget that the contract with the employer does not include permanent job security. And there is a strong tendency, when something does go wrong with the venture, when the job is threatened, for the employee to blame others rather than himself. This leads inevitably, since there are so many more employees than employers, for the former to seek protection against such risks from some outside agency. And in a democracy that means the state. This is quite a natural tendency, but it cannot be carried very far without stifling initiative; and it should always be remembered that it is based on an attempt to do what is ultimately impossible, namely, escape the unpleasant consequences of living in a risky world.

4. "The range and variety of government action that is, at least in principle, reconcilable with a free system is thus considerable." [4] Regulation aimed at preservation of health is perfectly legitimate, and this might even include, for example, the prohibition of night work. Though it should be kept within narrow limits, there is no reason, in principle, why there could not be some state enterprise. Even such things as parks, sports facilities, and theaters can legitimately be state owned, though such control should be exercised by local, not central governments. Some provision of social security may also be justified as a legitimate function of government.

Hayek proposes not that such activities be prohibited in principle but that careful attention be given to the expected problems government action entails and the alternative possibilities. For example, he notes that "What is objectionable is not state enterprise as such but state monopoly." [5] This notion certainly accords with European experience since his lines were written. Efficiency is much higher and arbitrary political intervention much lower in those nationalized firms that must compete on private markets than in those firms that have an effective monopoly of the supply of their product. In the area of social security, Hayek is not much moved by charges such as Friedman's that forced saving for a retirement pension is an intolerable intervention into personal liberty. Instead, he emphasizes the consequences of government operation of the system, the creation of a vast and complex and relatively inefficient bureaucracy, and the co-optation of expertise into the system, so that it is virtually impossible to find someone who is both critical of the system and understands its intricacies.

But on this subject perhaps the remark that most needs pondering is: "So far as the preservation of personal liberty is concerned, the division of labor between a legislature which merely says that this or that should be done and an administrative apparatus which is given exclusive power to carry out these instructions is the most dangerous arrangement possible." [6] The growing complexity of the executive bureaucracy in the United States and the diminishing ability of an overburdened Congress to subject it to effective control would seem to exemplify this "most dangerous arrangement."

5.   Von Humboldt, the great Prussian schoolmaster, created the generally admired Prussian school system in the eighteenth century. It was a highly centralized system, and it worked, in the sense that it created a very well-trained population and was thereby widely emulated. But were not the consequences for both Prussia and the world catastrophic? There must be more to education than the acquisition of useful skills if it is to serve the needs of a free society.[7]

6.   The Beveridge Report, submitted to the British Parliament toward the end of World War II, became a sort of bible for the creators, there and elsewhere, of the contemporary welfare state. In it are identified the "five giants" that the report's proposals are designed to slay: want, disease, ignorance, squalor, and idleness. They are all great evil giants, no question. The problem, of course, is with the proposals, not the targets. As Hayek puts it, the proposals have in practice only served to generate five more giants: inflation, paralyzing taxation, coercive unions, government-run education, and the arbitrary social-security bureaucracy. Furthermore, it seems that the rise of the five new giants is now serving to promote the growth rather than the demise of the other five. Thus again have liberal good intentions backfired.[8]

7.   Political philosophers are not much known for their sense of humor. Hayek confines his to an occasional footnote, as in this quote from the eighteenth-century French finance minister Turgot when apprised of a gentleman's proposal to institute an income tax: "One should execute the author, not the proposal."

8.   Running through the discussion of many of the above points, and others as well, is Hayek's central notion that the idea of distributive justice is the subversive concept that most threatens to undermine the functioning of a free society. "Freedom is inseparable from rewards which often have no connection with merit and are therefor felt to be unjust." [9] Hayek never quite articulates a theory of entitlements, such as Robert Nozick's, mentioned above in chapter 17. However, he is both persistent and effective in arguing the interminable difficulties when a patterned ideal of distribution becomes the object of public policy. In particular, he has this to say about welfare economics: "In judging adaptations to changed circumstances comparisons of the new with the former position are irrelevant." [10] The change in circumstances does not permit either a claim that all are benefited or the identification of those that are hurt so that they may be compen-

sated. This is why welfare economics has never provided a usable basis for the evaluation of alternative social policies. Entitlements are not affected by this caveat, however, for what is tested there are not the outcomes, in terms of supplies of goods and services to individuals, but rights, whether or not the change is a consequence of someone's rights being violated. A society, even a minimal state, has the means to deal with such violations, since the damaged individuals will themselves make their claims before the judiciary. This is the great distinction, the one that separates liberal and conservative economics.

9. This is Hayek quoting the French conservative de Jouvenal: "We are thus driven to three conclusions. The first is that the small society, the milieu in which man is first found, retains for him an infinite attraction; the next, that he undoubtedly goes to it to renew his strength; but, the last, that any attempt to graft the same features on a large society is utopian and leads to tyranny." [11] The point the two authors are making is central to the situation in the modern free society, which is that of a very large collection of individuals. For such a society, there is no escape from a set of relatively abstract rules governing individual behavior. An impersonal rule of law is the only basis for equal treatment. We are constantly drawn back to the principles of those smaller societies where a sense of community could pervade and where propinquity gave meaning to the discretionary exercise of power by its rulers. But that is a blueprint for disaster in the modern nation, and learning that lesson will be a major task not just for our generation but for future ones, as we gradually come to terms with our new situation.

In its discussion of the future, the last chapter of Part I provides the basis for an affirmative and optimistic conservative outlook. The roots of this optimism lie partly in the power of conservative arguments, partly in their durability in severe tests over a period of many generations, partly in the special confirmations that events of more recent times have provided, and partly in the obvious resurgence of conservatism as an intellectual movement, as a political movement, and as an orientation toward economic analysis. Karl Marx once said that the function of intellectual activity was not so much to understand the world as to change it. A conservative restatement of his remark may serve as the coda to the present work:

The key step in the analysis of social arrangements is to understand the severe limits imposed on any such analysis. We do not understand well how society works. However, we have learned through bitter experience that civilization is based on order, and that order is the basis of human freedom and material affluence. We have also learned that the individual is worthy of respect as an organism capable of assuming responsibility for his own actions. And we have learned that the market, essentially a system of voluntary agreements for the cooperative production and exchange of goods and services, allows the individual maximum responsibility. Bureaucrats are a necessary evil for only a very limited range of actions mostly associated with the preservation of public order and rights. The function of intellectual activity is to serve the individual's curiosity. Hopefully, an increasing number of intellectuals will attempt to persuade their fellow citizens that the world does not need coerced change so long as rights are secure.

Notes*

Chapter 2

1. Three works have played an important role in the development of this new interpretation of history. With magnificent sweep, William McNeill in his *The Rise of the West* (Chicago: University of Chicago Press, 1963),* tells the story of world history substantially in terms of the role of diffusion of better techniques and better forms of social organization from their points of origin around the world; and, of course, trade is a major facilitator of this process. Sir John Hicks, *A Theory of Economic History* (New York: Oxford University Press, 1969),* is the place to go to understand the central role of markets in the economic history of the West. Hicks, a Nobel Prize winner who turned from economic theory to history late in life, has clearly put a lifetime of reading, plus his grasp of economic theory, into this fundamental revision of the subject. For a challenging interpretation of the rise of the Western world in which the development of property rights plays a central role, see the book of that title by Douglass North and Robert Thomas (Cambridge: Cambridge University Press, 1973). Our account in this and the next two chapters draws heavily on the ideas contained in these works.

2. For an account of the substantial economic development of colonial Africa, see Peter Bauer's *West African Trade* (Cambridge: Cambridge University Press, 1954), and his other works cited in the Suggestions for Further Reading. Morris Morris, *Emergence of an Industrial Labor Force in India* (Berkeley: University of California Press, 1965), and elsewhere, shows that there were substantial positive benefits from colonial rule in this part of the world and that the asserted destruction of native handicrafts by the colonial regime simply did not occur.

3. Friedrich Hayek, ed., *Capitalism and the Historians* (Chicago: University of Chicago Press, 1954), provides the key essays in this revision of the economic history of the industrial revolution.

4. The central economic role of the family is a major thread in the works of Joseph Schumpeter. For a good example, see Part II of his *Capitalism, Socialism and Democracy* (New York: Harper, 1944).*

Chapter 3

1. Wolfram Eberhard's *A History of China,* 3rd ed. (Berkeley: University of California Press, 1969) provides many insights into Chinese history along the lines suggested in the text. Mark Elvin, *The Pattern of the Chinese Past* (Stanford: Stanford University Press, 1973),* offers further insights into the dynamism of Chinese society, technologically as well as organizationally. The first four chapters of Frederic Wakeman, *The Fall of Imperial China* (New York: Free Press, 1975), contains a succinct and very useful description of the gentry, the merchants, the peasants, and their interactions under the dynastic cycle.

2. A beautiful account of the significance of the Venetian republic is to be found in Frederick C. Lane's *Venice, A Maritime Republic* (Baltimore: Johns Hopkins University Press, 1973);* a nicely illustrated summa of Lane's lifetime of work on the topic. An extended account of the Venetian bureaucracy and welfare system is provided by Brian Pullan, *Rich and Poor in Renaissance Venice* (Cambridge: Harvard University Press, 1971).

* Starred items are available in paperback.

Notes

Chapter 4

1. This is the term used by Hicks in his *Theory of Economic History* (New York: Oxford University Press, 1969).* This work and North and Thomas, *Rise of the Western World* (Cambridge: Cambridge University Press, 1973), provide the basis for the historical interpretations of this chapter.
2. David Thomson's *England in the Nineteenth Century* (Harmondsworth, England: Pelican, 1959),* though not conservative in orientation, clearly shows the ways in which merchant-influenced government allowed and at times encouraged the rise of the thoroughgoing market economy, and the relation between both of these and the essentially peaceful process of transition to democracy.
3. For an account of the roles of markets and public order in the development of England, France, Japan and China, see Robert T. Holt and John Turner, *The Political Basis of Economic Development* (New York: Van Nostrand, 1966).*
4. Jonathan Hughes, *The Vital Few* (Boston: Houghton Mifflin, 1966), shows the special significance of individual efforts in the development of the American economy.
5. In thinking of the effects of the rising market system on general recognition of rights, one might note that after 1838 no one in England was hanged except for murder or its attempt. This process of reducing the excessive cruelty of the criminal law is associated in many countries with the rise of a system of property rights and markets. As we will see in chapter 10, liberals pushed beyond this reform to coddling of criminals as "victims of society" with the rise of the redistributive state in the twentieth century.
6. Though the United States, protected by distance from foreign threat, still had the security lesson to learn by hard experience in the changed military environment of the twentieth century.

Chapter 5

1. This cycle, and other features of nineteenth-century dynamics, are described in Arthur Gayer, W. Rostow, and A. Schwartz, *Growth and Fluctuations in the British Economy, 1750–1850*, 2 vols. (Oxford: Oxford University Press, 1953).
2. The serious study of the role of information in making economies work dates from Friedrich Hayek's seminal paper, "The Use of Knowledge in Society," *American Economic Review* 35 (September 1945). For a contemporary statement of the issues, see Armen Alchian and Harold Demsetz, "Production, Information Costs and Economic Organization," *American Economic Review* 62 (December 1972).
3. Early American market structures in their relation to changing transport costs are discussed in part 4, and esp. chap. 32, of Harold Williamson, ed., *Growth of the American Economy* (Englewood Cliffs, N.J.: Prentice-Hall, 1951).
4. For a sobering account of the way in which government has stimulated rather than inhibited monopoly, see Alan Greenspan, "Antitrust," in Ayn Rand, ed., *Capitalism: The Unknown Ideal* (New York: New American Library, 1966).*
5. For persuasive and very readable applications of these arguments see, among others, the chapters on prostitution, medical care, the automobile, and flooding Hell's Canyon in Douglass North and Roger Miller, *The Economics of Public Issues*, 3rd ed. (New York: Harper and Row, 1976).*

Chapter 6

1. These early writers, usually identified as members of the Institutionalist School of economics, had a profound appreciation of the need for stability and evolutionary change in social arrangements. They also had many interesting things to say about the interaction between law and the economy. Had they been willing to accept the usefulness of economic analysis in generating insights into this interaction (and the need for stability), their work would have been much more influential. For a sample work that still retains some interest, see John R. Commons, *The Legal Foundations of Capitalism* (New York: Macmillan, 1924).* To appreciate the change in quality wrought by property rights analysis, compare this work with Robert Posner, *Economic Analysis of Law* (Boston: Little, Brown, 1972).
2. A succinct characterization of the basis of property-rights theory can be found in Harold Demsetz, "Toward a Theory of Property Rights," *American Economic Review* 57 (May 1967).

3. From a careful study of the German archives, Alexander Dallin in his *German Rule in Russia* (New York: Macmillan, 1957) has told this still too little known story. As Dallin recounts, Ukrainian peasants greeted the Nazi invaders as liberators from the Soviet yoke—until they discovered that the Nazis, as well as their previous Russian overlords, appreciated the brutal possibilities inherent in collective serfdom.

4. On this see North and Thomas, *The Rise of the Western World* (Cambridge: Cambridge University Press, 1973).

5. Dow Votaw, *Modern Corporations* (Englewood Cliffs, N.J.: Prentice-Hall, 1965).*

6. With his usual prescience, Milton Friedman included rent controls and publicly subsidized housing construction on his 1962 list of government "bads," long before it had become a major public scandal (or rather before the more recent scandals). See also his account of the failures of public housing in *Capitalism and Freedom* (Chicago: University of Chicago Press, 1962),* pp. 178–81.

Chapter 7

1. William Niskanen, *Bureaucracy and Representative Government* (Chicago: Aldine, 1971).

2. For a short and unforgettable account of how government and property interact, read Henry Manne, "The Parable of the Parking Lot," which can be found in the Furobotn and Pejovich collection, *The Economics of Property Rights* (Cambridge, Mass.: Ballinger, 1974).

3. Daniel P. Moynihan, *The Politics of a Guaranteed Income* (New York: Random House, 1973).

4. Ronald Coase, "The Federal Communications Commission," *Journal of Law and Economics* 2 (October 1959). This is a classic article both in its treatment of the facts and in stimulating the development of property rights theory. It is reprinted in Furobotn and Pejovich, *The Economics of Property Rights.*

5. Economic analysis of law has been developing rapidly in recent years, as the reader of the book by that title by Robert Posner (Boston: Little Brown, 1972) will see. It provides a good analytic basis for the shift from executive-type to judiciary-type treatment of externalities advocated in the text.

Chapter 8

1. Milton Friedman's most controversial proposal in *Capitalism and Freedom* is probably that to abolish occupational licensure, and particularly for medical practitioners. There are, of course, halfway houses for those not prepared to take such dramatic action, for example by sanctioning the licensing of people with smaller amounts of training for limited purposes. Movement in this direction has already occurred in the gradual development of paramedic practice, something the armed services have long had.

2. Most of the problems associated with welfare and proliferating bureaucracies are tied up with large cities. For an excellent survey of what has been learned—and unlearned—by students of public policy in this area over the past two decades, see Edward Banfield, *The Unheavenly City Revisited* (Boston: Little, Brown, 1974).* See also the discussion in chapter 19 below.

3. For a typical statement in favor of the relative poverty concept, see Richard Titmuss, ed., *Essays on the Welfare State* (Boston: Beacon, 1969).* For some conservative thoughts on these matters, see William F. Buckley, Jr., *Four Reforms, A Program for the 70's* (New York: Putnam, 1973).

Chapter 9

1. This position is well argued in Milton Friedman and David Meiselman, "The Relative Stability of Monetary Velocity and the Investment Multiplier in the U.S. 1897–1958," in E. C. Brown, ed., *Stabilization Policies* (Englewood Cliffs, N.J.: Prentice-Hall, 1963), where the difficulties with the multiplier concept are pointed out. An empirical test reveals that the multiplier is a far from constant "constant,"

and the monetarist concept of velocity is shown to be both empirically and theoretically a more satisfying base for policy analysis.

2. A considerable minority of economists was never sold on Keynesianism. Over the last decade or so the number of dissidents has been increasing rapidly. One of the seminal books in the debate was Axel Leijonhufvud's, *Keynesian Economics and the Economics of Keynes* (New York: Oxford University Press, 1968). For a short and lucid discussion of major issues, chap. 3 of Friedman's *Capitalism and Freedom* is still hard to beat.

3. Milton Friedman and Anna Schwartz's magisterial *A Monetary History of the United States* (Princeton: Princeton University Press, 1963), provides overwhelming documentation in support of the thesis that the single most productive measure for dealing with monetary instability would be to prevent continuing monetary mismanagement by removing most discretionary authority from the hands of government officials.

4. See chapter 3 above and particularly Frederick C. Lane's *Venice, A Maritime Republic* (Baltimore: Johns Hopkins University Press, 1973),* pp. 331–34 and 430. After the Venetian nobility shifted from trade to landowning as the basis of its wealth, the size of the nobility declined and wealth became more concentrated within the nobility. But a whole new class of merchant outsiders arose and prospered. Had they been fully accepted into the society, Venice might still be around! At the very least, the indications are that a late seventeenth- or eighteenth-century distribution of income that included these outsiders—who lived and worked in Venice—would not have been so different from earlier times.

Chapter 10

1. The distinction between ends-connectedness and means-connectedness is presented and analyzed in Hayek's new book, *The Mirage of Social Justice* (London: Routledge & Kegan Paul, 1976).

2. Probably the best general account of how revolutions come about is still Lyford Edwards, *The Natural History of Revolution* (Chicago: University of Chicago Press, 1927). Though rather old, this book avoids Crane Brinton's mistake of trying to equate the American with the Russian revolution (*Anatomy of Revolution* [New York: Norton, 1938]). Thomas Greene, *Comparative Revolutionary Movements* (Englewood Cliffs, N.J.: Prentice-Hall, 1974), is somewhat tainted by sociological jargon, but clearly shows the tendency for leaders of the left to be scions of the upper class, and so more distant from their followers than are the leaders of other movements. Greene also shows the association between the unwillingness or inability of governments to act and the success of revolution.

3. For a very good account of the relations between crime and social policy, see chap. 8 of Edward Banfield, *The Unheavenly City Revisited* (Boston: Little, Brown, 1974).*

Chapter 11

1. A scholarly account of the economic achievements of Taiwan is provided in a forthcoming study by Walter Galenson and Nai-ruenn Chen.

2. The annual surveys of the *Far Eastern Economic Review* provide ample evidence of the performance of these two trading economies. Keith Hopkins, ed., *Hong Kong, The Industrial Economy,* (New York: Oxford University Press, 1971),* demonstrates the reluctant admiration liberals express at the success of conservative monetary and fiscal policy in Hong Kong.

3. Stanley Wellisz, "Lessons of Twenty Years of Planning in Developing Countries," *Economica* 38, n.s. (May 1971), explains the rather dramatic downward reassessment by liberal economists of the effectiveness of planning. I.M.D. Little and Tibor Scitovsky, *Industry and Trade in Some Developing Countries: A Comparative Study* (New York: Oxford University Press, 1970), have produced a scholarly, negative assessment of the effects of policies of import substitution.

4. The economist who has devoted his professional career to demonstrating, in the face of almost universal academic disbelief and even hostility, that the market and free enterprise works in the "Third World" as well as elsewhere, is Peter Bauer. The range of his thought on this subject is well captured in his collection of essays, *Dissent on Development* (Cambridge: Harvard University Press, 1972). He colloborated with Basil Yamey in writing *The Economics of Underdeveloped Countries* (Chicago: University of Chicago Press, 1957).

5. Holt and Turner, *The Political Basis of Economic Development* (New York: Van Nostrand, 1966),* discuss the political aspects of the early development efforts.
6. This tubewell story was told in a lecture at Berkeley a few years ago by economist Robert Dorfman, who worked for a time in Pakistan for the Development Advisory Service of Harvard.

Chapter 12

1. Friedman's ideas are expounded in chap. 4 of *Capitalism and Freedom,* and the events leading up to the float are analyzed in chap. 5 of his *An Economist's Protest.*
2. Joseph Schumpeter in his essay, "Imperialism" (published in English in Schumpeter: *Imperialism and Social Classes* [New York: Meridian, 1960]) provides an account of imperialist behavior that puts the role of the market and of the businessman in a proper perspective. Though forty years old, it may still be the best thing available on the subject.
3. For a good account of Chilean copper, which evaluates the effects of the copper companies' operations on the Chilean economy, see Clark Reynolds and M. Mamalakis, *Essays on the Chilean Economy* (Homewood, Ill.: Irwin, 1965), the essay by Reynolds being the relevant one.
4. Peter Bauer and Basil Yamey, *The Economics of Underdeveloped Countries* (Chicago: University of Chicago Press, 1957), provide evidence in favor of these assertions for colonial governments.
5. For an account of this waste in the case of aid to Greece, see William Mc-Neill, *American Aid in Action 1947–1956* (New York: Twentieth Century Fund, 1957).

Chapter 13

1. Thanks to Frank Knight and Michael Polanyi, a good basic perspective on the idea of socialism can be acquired rather quickly: see Knight's "Socialism: The Nature of the Problem," reprinted as chap. 5 in his *Freedom and Reform* (New York: Harper, 1947), and Polanyi's "Towards a Theory of Conspicuous Production," *Soviet Survey,* October 1960. George Halm, *Economic Systems, A Comparative Analysis,* 3rd ed. (New York: Holt, 1968), offers a thoughtful account of the development of twentieth-century socialism.
2. Another disturbing aspect of socialism has been developed by Frederick Pryor in his *Public Expenditures in Communist and Capitalist Nations* (New Haven: Yale University Press, 1968). He offers a striking demonstration of the similarities in public policy attitudes of liberals and radicals by showing that most of the time the patterns of public expenditures in the two types of economies are statistically indistinguishable. The difference between liberals and radicals actually is not all that great.
3. For a solid account of its workings in the Soviet Union, see Gregory Grossman, "The Soviet Second Economy," *Problems of Communism* 26 (Sept./Oct. 1977), pp. 25–40.
4. This and other assertions about Czechoslovakia are a product of the author's visit to that country during the "Prague spring."

Chapter 14

1. There does not seem to be a good analysis of the international order along conservative lines. It is unfortunate though understandable that Hayek has explicitly excluded it from consideration in his massive works on political theory. However, the basic notions used in discussing domestic order seem to be transferable to the international scene with little modification.
2. For example, in the later years of the authoritarian Salazar regime in Portugal, even the works of French communists were available, in Portuguese translation, in bookstores.
3. Albert Wohlstetter in "Racing Forward or Ambling Back," in *Defending America* (New York: Basic Books, 1977), lays out the options on this central topic.

Chapter 15

1. Joe S. Bain, in his *Environmental Decay, Economic Causes and Remedies* (Boston: Little, Brown, 1973) shows how one initial measure, for reduced compression ratios on certain cars, probably led to increased pollution.

Chapter 16

1. Freedom and family have always been central concerns of conservative thought. The major development in that thought over time, aside from the steady process of enrichment of the basic ideas through continuing accumulation of experience, has been the strong trend toward increasing the scope of freedom. The original notions were closely associated with preserving the freedoms of aristocratic families against the depredations of kings and emperors. But as time went on and social and economic development continued, it became feasible to expand the range of the population that could be included within the basic framework of freedom. The great English philosophers of the seventeenth and eighteenth centuries were concerned to bring the solid citizenry, gentry, and merchants, within the framework; the American revolution was largely inspired by these notions, together with their French counterparts. But a still larger expansion occurred in the nineteenth century as a whole series of thinkers began coming to terms with the potential of the thoroughgoing market economy. Roughly speaking, this revolutionary expansion in the applicability of conservatism was expected to embrace all those citizens of a country who were prepared to accept the established market-democratic political process as the definer of the framework of economic and political activity.

This long tradition must be sharply distinguished from another conservatizing tradition, namely, the organicists, who tended to give the state some sort of mystical identity and to think of individuals as functional parts of this larger, organic whole. That line of belief was typically associated with hierarchic societies, and is a very different thing from the drive for independence of control by others that is the cornerstone of the conservative tradition we are following in this work. The reader interested in conservatism's more distant forebears can do no better than read Friedrich A. Hayek's *The Constitution of Liberty* (Chicago: University of Chicago Press, 1962).

2. George N. Nash's extremely useful *The Conservative Intellectual Movement in America Since 1945* (New York: Basic Books, 1976), provides an overview that emphasizes the trends toward coalescence and divergence of the various strands of conservative thought. The bibliographical notes to that book give the reader an idea of the volume and scope of conservative writings, and guides to selection.

3. Frank Meyer's role as advocate for fusion among conservatives is described in chap. 6 of Nash, *Conservative Intellectual Movement*. Our optimal conservative is clearly a fusionist, though the specific arguments differ somewhat.

4. As Nash, *Conservative Intellectual Movement*, notes, Walter Lippmann's *An Inquiry Into the Principles of the Good Society* (Boston: Little, Brown, 1937) was a major stimulus to the eventual founding of the Mont Pélerin Society.

Chapter 17

1. James Buchanan's general orientation can be found in part IV of his and Gordon Tullock's *The Calculus of Consent* (Ann Arbor: University of Michigan Press, 1962). For a variety of applications of his mode of economic analysis to problems of public choice, see his *Demand and Supply of Public Goods* (Chicago: Rand McNally, 1968).

2. A glance at *Man, Economy and the State*, 2 vols. (New York: Van Nostrand, 1962) or *Power and the Market, Government and the Economy* (Menlo Park, Calif.: Institute for Humane Studies, Inc., 1970),* will convince the reader that Murray Rothbard is the purest of the pure libertarian breed.

3. Robert Posner, *Economic Analysis of Law* (Boston: Little, Brown, 1972).

4. Robert Nozick, *Anarchy, State, and Utopia* (New York: Basic Books, 1974).

5. We should not leave this topic without mentioning Ayn Rand, whose works do not contain much economics but are certainly stimulating. Of her two principal novels, *Fountainhead* (New York: Bobbs-Merrill, 1943) * and *Atlas Shrugged* (New York: Random House, 1957),* I believe the former to be the more interesting and relevant to the conservative economic world view.

Chapter 18

1. The great book in this genre, from the point of view of economics at least, is Joseph Schumpeter's *Capitalism, Socialism and Democracy* (New York: Harper, 1944). The work includes, in addition to a broad-gauge account of capitalism's historical dynamics, a theory of democracy that has served as the basis for much later work, a brilliant account of Marx's thought, and an analysis of socialist political movements. The starting point for postwar traditionalist conservatism in the United States is Russell Kirk's *The Conservative Mind* (Chicago: Regnery, 1960).

2. For an influential political philosophy, see Leo Strauss's *Natural Right and History* (Chicago: University of Chicago Press, 1953) and more recent *Political Philosophy and the Issues of Politics* (Chicago: University of Chicago Press, 1977) by his student Joseph Cropsey. A contemporary sociologist who fits reasonably well into this mold and writes persuasively is Robert Nisbet, whose *Quest for Community* (New York: Oxford University Press, 1953), and *The Twilight of Authority* (New York: Oxford University Press, 1975), are perhaps his most interesting efforts. Nash, *The Conservative Intellectual Movement in America Since 1945* (New York: Basic Books, 1976), offers a number of additional suggestions. William F. Buckley, Jr.'s magazine, *National Review*, provides wit and argument that falls mostly within this genre, but unfortunately gives relatively little weight to the economic side.

Chapter 19

1. Perhaps the single best place to go to get the general line of argument of members of this group is Edward Banfield's *The Unheavenly City Revisited* (Boston: Little, Brown, 1974).* Though Banfield does not seem to be a "recusant liberal," his views are quite close to where the others are tending, and though he is a political scientist rather than an economist, he emphasizes in his writing aspects of urban life that are economically relevant. The first five of our six points describing neoconservative views are taken from this work. Daniel Patrick Moynihan's more recent works, including *The Politics of a Guaranteed Income* (New York: Random House, 1973) and *Maximum Feasible Misunderstanding* (New York: Free Press, 1969), Nathan Glazer's *Remembering the Answer: Essays on the American Student Revolt* (New York: Basic Books, 1970), and Irving Kristol's *On the Democratic Idea in America* (New York: Harper and Row, 1972), are central works in the genre. The quarterly *Public Interest* is a sort of unofficial gazette of this group and regularly includes pieces dealing with the economy.

2. Of course, to be future-oriented does not imply that one must favor a policy of governmental attempts to increase the longer-run rate of growth. Ezra Mishan, *Technology and Growth, The Price We Pay* (New York: Praeger, 1970), represents effectively the economist who feels that growth is tending to become too costly in terms of amenities foregone.

Chapter 20

1. Friedman has, of course, become a Nobel laureate. His writings of special interest for the purposes of this book have already been cited a number of times. It might be noted here, just as a reminder, that Friedman as a leading professional economist has produced a large body of writings at a more technical level, and that these are the basis for his reputation within the profession. But, of course, the two genres are connected, and in Friedman's case they form a mutually compatible whole. The specific issues raised in this chapter are all discussed in *Capitalism and Freedom*, especially in chaps. 6 and 11. The list of steps proposed in reforming the international monetary system appear in chap. 4 of the same work.

Chapter 21

1. Frederich A. Hayek, *The Constitution of Liberty* (Chicago: University of Chicago Press, 1962), p. 62.

2. Ibid., p. 61.

3. Ibid., p. 62.

4. Ibid., p. 123.

5. Ibid., p. 231.

6. Ibid., p. 224.

7. See ibid., pp. 378–79 for a discussion of Humboldt.

8. See ibid., pp. 305 and 516n. 2 for a discussion of the Beveridge Report.

9. Fredrich A. Hayek, *The Mirage of Social Justice* (London: Routledge & Kegan Paul, 1976), p. 120.

10. Hayek, *Constitution of Liberty*, p. 261.

11. Hayek, *Mirage of Social Justice*, p. 191n. 15.

Suggestions for Further Reading*

Alchian, Armin, and William Allen. *University Economics,* 2nd ed. Belmont, Calif.: Wadsworth, 1968.
> From a conservative perspective, probably the best full-scale principles textbook on the market.

Banfield, Edward. *The Unheavenly City Revisited.* Boston: Houghton Mifflin, 1974.*
> A first-rate account of the successes and failures (mostly the latter) of government policies with respect to the cities, welfare, and so on, and a very plausible explanation as to why such policies by their nature can have little effect on the problems.

Bauer, Peter, and Basil Yamey. *The Economics of Underdeveloped Countries.* Chicago: University of Chicago Press, 1957.
> A treatise on development whose first author is perhaps the most distinguished contemporary student of the subject in the conservative tradition.

Black, Angus (pseud.). *A Radical's Guide to Economic Reality.* New York: Holt, Rinehart and Winston, 1970.*
> A sort of "Chicago School" put-on. What is radical about this 100-page book is that, in contrast to the radical diatribes that were so popular at the time of its publication, it takes the market seriously as a resource allocator. In these liberal days that is in fact radical.

Buchanan, James, and Gordon Tullock. *The Calculus of Consent.* Ann Arbor: University of Michigan Press, 1962.*
> Another classic that characterizes what might be called the position of contractarian anarchism.

Friedman, Milton. *Capitalism and Freedom.* Chicago: University of Chicago Press, 1962.*
> A classic survey and analysis of major public policy issues. Though it deals explicitly with the issues of its day, it seems to have become increasingly relevant over the years.

Friedman, Milton. *An Economist's Protest.* Glen Ridge, N.J.: Horton, 1972.*
> A collection of Friedman's essays taken from *Newsweek,* and consistently applying his ideas to current economic events.

Furobotn, Eirik, and Svetozar Pejovich, eds. *The Economics of Property Rights.* Cambridge, Mass.: Ballinger, 1974.
> A collection of some of the best writings on property-rights analysis in recent years, including the main essays on the subject cited in our footnotes.

Hayek, Friedrich, A. *The Constitution of Liberty.* Chicago: University of Chicago Press, 1962.
> Hayek's magnum opus, a powerful integration of both the political and economic ideas of conservatism.

———. *Studies in Philosophy, Politics and Economics.* Chicago: University of Chicago Press, 1967.*
> Chap. 11 in this collection of essays is entitled "The Principles of a Liberal Social Order." It provides a comprehensive list of those principles and succinct commentary.

——— *Law, Legislation and Liberty.*
> This is a projected three-volume treatise of which the first two volumes, *Rules and Order,* London: Routledge & Kegan Paul, 1973, and *The Mirage of Social Justice,* London: Routledge & Kegan Paul, 1976, have already appeared. Though dealing more with law and political theory than with economics, they represent Hayek's latest thinking on the interrelation among these three, and the second volume is an especially useful refutation of contemporary liberal theories of justice.

Holt, Robert T., and John Turner. *The Political Basis of Economic Development.* New York: Van Nostrand, 1966.*
> Emphasizes the role of governmental nonacton in contributing to the early

* Starred items are available in paperback edition.

stages of economic development, taking evidence from pre-twentieth-century economies.

Kirk, Russell. *The Conservative Mind.* Chicago: Regnery, 1960.
> The starting point for postwar traditionalist conservatism in the United States. Interesting in that Kirk combines this version of conservatism with a relatively libertarian attitude toward the economy.

Knight, Frank. *Freedom and Reform.* New York: Harper, 1947.
> A collection of essays by the great Chicago teacher. The essay "Freedom as Fact and Criterion" is most percipient on this issue and its relevance for economics. The same can be said for "Socialism: The Nature of the Problem."

Nash, George N. *The Conservative Intellectual Movement in America Since 1945.* New York: Basic Books, 1976.
> An excellent, detailed, and dispassionate account of the subject.

North, Douglass, and Roger Miller. *The Economics of Public Issues,* 3rd ed. New York: Harper and Row, 1976.*
> An introductory survey of economic issues viewed from the property-rights perspective, it provides a very good and brief introduction to economic analysis that is fully compatible with conservative principles.

North, Douglass, and Robert Thomas. *The Rise of the Western World: A New Economic History.* Cambridge: University of Cambridge Press, 1973.
> Tells the story of the transformation of medieval into modern Europe in terms of the development of property rights.

Nozick, Robert. *Anarchy, State and Utopia.* New York: Basic Books, 1974.
> Defends the "minimal state" and argues cogently that there cannot be any connection between the idea of justice and the idea of a morally correct distribution of income or wealth.

Posner, Robert. *Economic Analysis of Law.* Boston: Little, Brown, 1972.
> An already classic work that uses the new property-rights theory and economic theory to analyze legal concepts in terms of their efficiency, as measured on the market.

Rothbard, Murray. *Power and the Market, Government and the Economy.* Menlo Park, Calif.: Institute for Humane Studies, 1970.*
> The libertarian position carried to its extreme limit, where it merges with anarchy.

Schumpeter, Joseph. *Capitalism, Socialism and Democracy.* New York: Harper, 1944.
> A classic work on the dynamics of capitalism, and on the stultifying effects of socialism, written by one of the great conservative economists of this century. It is perhaps understandable, given the time of writing, that he was unduly pessimistic as to capitalism's future.

————. *Imperialism and Social Classes.* New York: Meridian, 1960.*
> Another of Schumpeter's classic accounts of a much-misunderstood phenomenon.

Thomson, David. *England in the Nineteenth Century.* Harmondsworth, England: Pelican, 1959.*
> Without being conservative in orientation, it tells the conservative story of the inseparable connections between economic progress, freedom, and order in the development of the thoroughgoing market economy.

Index

Abandoned buildings, 36
Albania, Western socialists and, 18
Alchian, Armen, 130
Allende, Salvatore, 85
American Medical Association, 49
Anarchism, libertarian conservatism and, 104
Anarchy, State and Utopia (Nozick), 106
Anglo-American common law, 44
Angola, cause of revolution in, 60
Anticommunism, 98
Argentina, internal violence in, 84
Arbitration of property disputes, 35–36
Athens, 8, 10; military defense of, 90
Austria, standard of living in, 80–81
Authoritarian regimes, 84–86
Automobile industry: environmentalism and, 92; foreign competition in, 73
Aztecs, 10

Bain, Joe S., 134
Banfield, Edward, 131, 132, 135
Bauer, Peter, 129, 132, 133
Berlin crisis, 100
Beveridge Report, 125
Blacks, individual policy effects related to, 115
Boulton, William, 23
Brazil: authoritarian regime in, 85; development in, 65
Brinton, Crane, 132
Britain: class warfare in, 61; emergence as trading nation of, 8, 10; feudal, 13; foreign investments by, 73; health care in, 47; international money market and, 71; laissez-faire economy in, 15; monopolies in, 29; ownership of means of production in, 37; patent law in, 35; principle

of freedom in, 97; restrictions on trade by American colonies of, 72; rise of modern industry in, 21–25; rise of real wages in, 12; short-period business cycles in, 27; welfare system in, 125
Brown, E. C., 131
Brown, Jerry, 41
Buchanan, James, 102–4, 134
Buckley, William F., Jr., 131, 135
Bulgaria, authoritarian regime in, 85
Bureaucracy: in ancient China, 16–17; information and, 9; law vs., 43–46; mode of functioning of, 39–40; property rights and, 41–43; Venetian, 18–19
Byzantium, 8, 10

Carter, Jimmy, 55
Carthage, 16
Castro, Fidel, 81
Chicago, University of, 28
Chicago School, 109
Chile: authoritarian regime in, 84–85; copper mines in, 73–74; landowners in, 68
California: state budget of, 40; tax rates in, 55
Capital market, improved functioning of, 24
China: ancient, 16–17, 49, 108; cause of revolution in, 60; development in, 64–65; health care in, 47–48; illegal trade in, 79; internal violence in, 84; military capability of, 86; property rights and, 37; Western socialists and, 81
Civil War, 59
Class warfare, 61
Club of Rome, 93
Coase, Ronald, 131